LETTER OF TRANSMITTAL

BOARD OF GOVERNORS OF THE
FEDERAL RESERVE SYSTEM

Washington, D.C., February 24, 2015

THE PRESIDENT OF THE SENATE
THE SPEAKER OF THE HOUSE OF REPRESENTATIVES

The Board of Governors is pleased to submit its *Monetary Policy Report* pursuant to section 2B of the Federal Reserve Act.

Sincerely,

Janet L. Yellen

Janet L. Yellen, Chair

STATEMENT ON LONGER-RUN GOALS AND MONETARY POLICY STRATEGY

Adopted effective January 24, 2012; as amended effective January 27, 2015

The Federal Open Market Committee (FOMC) is firmly committed to fulfilling its statutory mandate from the Congress of promoting maximum employment, stable prices, and moderate long-term interest rates. The Committee seeks to explain its monetary policy decisions to the public as clearly as possible. Such clarity facilitates well-informed decisionmaking by households and businesses, reduces economic and financial uncertainty, increases the effectiveness of monetary policy, and enhances transparency and accountability, which are essential in a democratic society.

Inflation, employment, and long-term interest rates fluctuate over time in response to economic and financial disturbances. Moreover, monetary policy actions tend to influence economic activity and prices with a lag. Therefore, the Committee's policy decisions reflect its longer-run goals, its medium-term outlook, and its assessments of the balance of risks, including risks to the financial system that could impede the attainment of the Committee's goals.

The inflation rate over the longer run is primarily determined by monetary policy, and hence the Committee has the ability to specify a longer-run goal for inflation. The Committee reaffirms its judgment that inflation at the rate of 2 percent, as measured by the annual change in the price index for personal consumption expenditures, is most consistent over the longer run with the Federal Reserve's statutory mandate. Communicating this inflation goal clearly to the public helps keep longer-term inflation expectations firmly anchored, thereby fostering price stability and moderate long-term interest rates and enhancing the Committee's ability to promote maximum employment in the face of significant economic disturbances. The maximum level of employment is largely determined by nonmonetary factors that affect the structure and dynamics of the labor market. These factors may change over time and may not be directly measurable. Consequently, it would not be appropriate to specify a fixed goal for employment; rather, the Committee's policy decisions must be informed by assessments of the maximum level of employment, recognizing that such assessments are necessarily uncertain and subject to revision. The Committee considers a wide range of indicators in making these assessments. Information about Committee participants' estimates of the longer-run normal rates of output growth and unemployment is published four times per year in the FOMC's Summary of Economic Projections. For example, in the most recent projections, FOMC participants' estimates of the longer-run normal rate of unemployment had a central tendency of 5.2 percent to 5.5 percent.

In setting monetary policy, the Committee seeks to mitigate deviations of inflation from its longer-run goal and deviations of employment from the Committee's assessments of its maximum level. These objectives are generally complementary. However, under circumstances in which the Committee judges that the objectives are not complementary, it follows a balanced approach in promoting them, taking into account the magnitude of the deviations and the potentially different time horizons over which employment and inflation are projected to return to levels judged consistent with its mandate.

The Committee intends to reaffirm these principles and to make adjustments as appropriate at its annual organizational meeting each January.

Contents

NOTE: Unless otherwise noted, the time series in the figures extend through, for daily data, February 19, 2015; for monthly data, January 2015; and, for quarterly data, 2014:Q4. In bar charts, except as noted, the change for a given period is measured to its final quarter from the final quarter of the preceding period.

Summary

The labor market improved further during the second half of last year and into early 2015, and labor market conditions moved closer to those the Federal Open Market Committee (FOMC) judges consistent with its maximum employment mandate. Since the middle of last year, monthly payrolls have expanded by about 280,000, on average, and the unemployment rate has declined nearly ½ percentage point on net. Nevertheless, a range of labor market indicators suggest that there is still room for improvement. In particular, at 5.7 percent, the unemployment rate is still above most FOMC participants' estimates of its longer-run normal level, the labor force participation rate remains below most assessments of its trend, an unusually large number of people continue to work part time when they would prefer full-time employment, and wage growth has continued to be slow.

A steep drop in crude oil prices since the middle of last year has put downward pressure on overall inflation. As of December 2014, the price index for personal consumption expenditures was only ¾ percent higher than a year earlier, a rate of increase that is well below the FOMC's longer-run goal of 2 percent. Even apart from the energy sector, price increases have been subdued. Indeed, the prices of items other than food and energy products rose at an annual rate of only about 1 percent over the last six months of 2014, noticeably less than in the first half of the year. The slow pace of price increases during the second half was likely associated, in part, with falling import prices and perhaps also with some pass-through of lower oil prices. Survey-based measures of longer-term inflation expectations have remained stable; however market-based measures of inflation compensation have declined since last summer.

Economic activity expanded at a strong pace in the second half of last year. Notably reflecting solid gains in consumer spending, real gross domestic product (GDP) is estimated to have increased at an annual rate of 3¾ percent after a reported increase of just 1¼ percent in the first half of the year. The growth in GDP was supported by accommodative monetary policy, a reduction in the degree of restraint imparted by fiscal policy, and the increase in households' purchasing power arising from the drop in oil prices. The gains in GDP have occurred despite continued sluggish growth abroad and a sizable appreciation of the U.S. dollar, both of which have weighed on net exports.

Financial conditions in the United States have generally remained supportive of economic growth. Longer-term interest rates in the United States and other advanced economies have continued to move down, on net, since the middle of 2014 amid disappointing economic growth and low inflation abroad as well as the associated anticipated and actual monetary policy actions by foreign central banks. Broad indexes of U.S. equity prices have risen moderately, on net, since the end of June. Credit flows to nonfinancial businesses largely remained solid in the second half of last year. Overall borrowing conditions for households eased further, but mortgage lending standards are still tight for many potential borrowers.

The vulnerability of the U.S. financial system to financial instability has remained moderate, primarily reflecting low-to-moderate levels of leverage and maturity transformation. Asset valuation pressures have eased a little, on balance, but continue to be notable in some sectors. The capital and liquidity positions of the banking sector have improved further. Over the second half of 2014, the Federal Reserve and other agencies finalized or proposed several more rules related to the Dodd-Frank Wall Street Reform and Consumer Protection Act of 2010, which were designed to further strengthen the resilience of the financial system.

At the time of the FOMC meeting in late January of this year, the Committee saw the outlook as broadly similar to that at the time of its December meeting, when the most recent Summary of Economic Projections (SEP) was compiled. (The December SEP is included as Part 3 of this report.) The FOMC expects that, with appropriate monetary policy accommodation, economic activity will expand at a moderate pace, and that labor market indicators will continue to move toward levels the Committee judges consistent with its dual mandate of maximum employment and price stability. In addition, the Committee continues to see the risks to the outlook for economic activity and the labor market as nearly balanced. Inflation is anticipated to decline further in the near term, mainly reflecting the pass-through of lower oil prices to consumer energy prices. However, the Committee expects inflation to rise gradually toward its 2 percent longer-run objective over the medium term as the labor market improves further and the transitory effects of lower energy prices and other factors dissipate.

At the end of October, and after having made further measured reductions in the pace of its asset purchases at its July and September meetings, the FOMC concluded the asset purchase program that began in September 2012. The decision to end the purchase program reflected the substantial improvement in the outlook for the labor market since the program's inception—the stated aim of the asset purchases—and a judgment that the underlying strength of the broader economy was sufficient to support ongoing progress toward the Committee's policy objectives.

Nonetheless, the Committee continued to judge that a high degree of policy accommodation remained appropriate. As a result, the FOMC has maintained the exceptionally low target range of 0 to ¼ percent for the federal funds rate and kept the Federal Reserve's holdings of longer-term securities at sizable levels. The Committee has also continued to provide forward guidance bearing on the anticipated path of the federal funds rate. In particular, the FOMC has stressed that in deciding how long to maintain the current target range, it will consider a broad set of indicators to assess realized and expected progress toward its objectives. On the basis of its assessment, the Committee indicated in its two most recent postmeeting statements that it can be patient in beginning to normalize the stance of monetary policy.

To further emphasize the data-dependent nature of its policy stance, the FOMC has stated that if incoming information indicates faster progress toward its policy objectives than the Committee currently expects, increases in the target range for the federal funds rate will likely occur sooner than the Committee anticipates. The FOMC has also indicated that in the case of slower-than-expected progress, increases in the target range will likely occur later than currently anticipated. Moreover, the Committee continues to expect that, even after employment and inflation are near mandate-consistent levels, economic conditions may, for some time, warrant keeping the target federal funds rate below levels the Committee views as normal in the longer run.

As part of prudent planning, the Federal Reserve has continued to prepare for the eventual normalization of the stance and conduct of monetary policy. The FOMC announced updated principles and plans for the normalization process following its September meeting and has continued to test the operational readiness of its monetary policy tools. The Committee remains confident that it has the tools it needs to raise short-term interest rates when doing so becomes appropriate, despite the very large size of the Federal Reserve's balance sheet.

PART 1
RECENT ECONOMIC AND FINANCIAL DEVELOPMENTS

The labor market continued to improve in the second half of last year and early this year. Job gains have averaged close to 280,000 per month since June, and the unemployment rate fell from 6.1 percent in June to 5.7 percent in January. Even so, the labor market likely has not yet fully recovered, and wage growth has remained slow. Since June, a steep drop in crude oil prices has exerted downward pressure on overall inflation, and non-energy price increases have been subdued as well. The price index for personal consumption expenditures (PCE) increased only ¾ percent during the 12 months ending in December, a rate that is well below the Federal Open Market Committee's (FOMC) longer-run objective of 2 percent; the index excluding food and energy prices was up 1¼ percent over this period. Survey measures of longer-run inflation expectations have been stable, but measures of inflation compensation derived from financial market quotes have moved down. Meanwhile, real gross domestic product (GDP) increased at an estimated annual rate of 3¾ percent in the second half of the year, up from a reported rate of just 1¼ percent in the first half. The growth in GDP has been supported by accommodative monetary policy and generally favorable financial conditions, the boost to households' purchasing power from lower oil prices, and improving consumer and business confidence. However, housing market activity has been advancing only slowly, and sluggish growth abroad and the higher foreign exchange value of the dollar have weighed on net exports. Longer-term interest rates in the United States and other advanced economies declined, on net, amid disappointing growth and low inflation abroad and the associated actual and anticipated accommodative monetary policy actions by foreign central banks.

Domestic Developments

The labor market has strengthened further . . .

Employment rose appreciably and the unemployment rate fell in the second half of 2014 and early this year. Payroll employment has increased by an average of about 280,000 per month since June, almost 40,000 faster than in the first half of last year (figure 1). The gain in payroll employment for 2014 as a whole was the largest for any year since 1999. In addition, the unemployment rate continued to move down, declining from 6.1 percent in June to 5.7 percent in January of this year, a rate more than 4 percentage points below its peak in 2009. Furthermore, a substantial portion of the decline in unemployment over the past year came from a decrease in the number of individuals reporting unemployment spells longer than six months.

The labor force participation rate has been roughly flat since late 2013 after having

declined not only during the recession, but also during much of the recovery period when most other indicators of labor market health were improving (figure 2). While much of that decline likely reflected ongoing demographic trends—such as the aging of members of the baby-boom generation into their retirement years—some of the decline likely

1. Net change in payroll employment

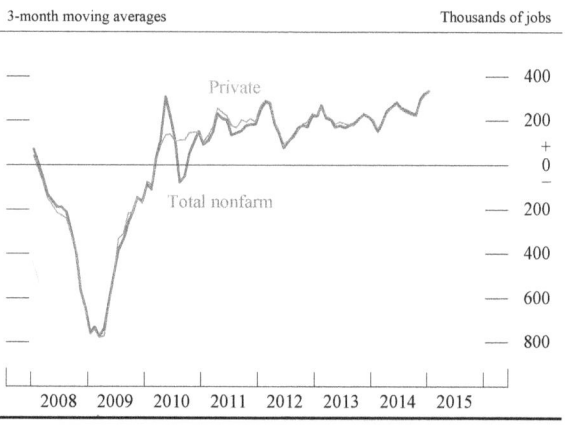

SOURCE: Department of Labor, Bureau of Labor Statistics.

2. Labor force participation rate and
    employment-to-population ratio

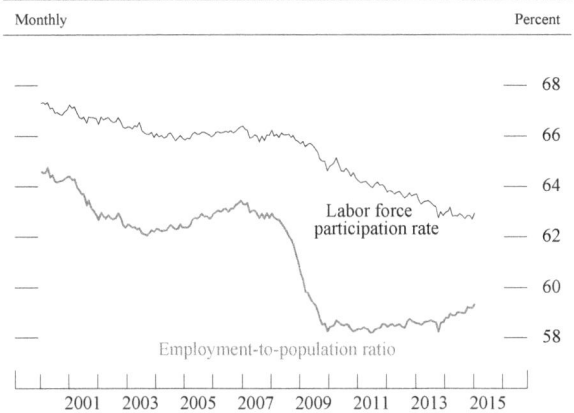

NOTE: Both series are a percent of the population aged 16 and over.
SOURCE: Department of Labor, Bureau of Labor Statistics.

reflected workers' perceptions of poor job opportunities. Judged against the backdrop of a declining trend, the recent stability of the participation rate likely represents some cyclical improvement. Nevertheless, the participation rate remains lower than would be expected given the unemployment rate, and thus it continues to suggest more cyclical weakness than is indicated by the unemployment rate.

Another sign that the labor market remains weaker than indicated by the unemployment rate alone is the still-elevated share of workers who are employed part time but would like to work full time. This share of involuntary part-time employees has generally shown less improvement than the unemployment rate over the past few years; in part for this reason, the more comprehensive U-6 measure of labor underutilization remains quite elevated (figure 3).

Nevertheless, most broad measures of labor market health have improved. With employment rising and the participation

3. Measures of labor underutilization

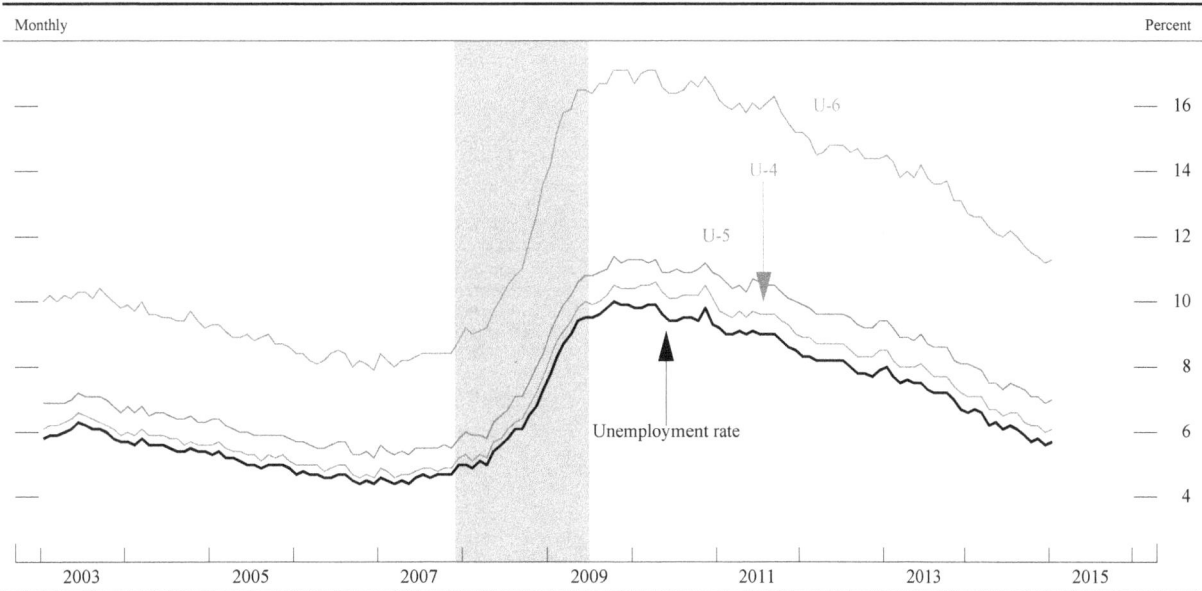

NOTE: U-4 measures total unemployed plus discouraged workers, as a percent of the labor force plus discouraged workers. Discouraged workers are a subset of marginally attached workers who are not currently looking for work because they believe no jobs are available for them. U-5 measures total unemployed plus all marginally attached to the labor force, as a percent of the labor force plus persons marginally attached to the labor force. Marginally attached workers are not in the labor force, want and are available for work, and have looked for a job in the past 12 months. U-6 measures total unemployed plus all marginally attached workers plus total employed part time for economic reasons, as a percent of the labor force plus all marginally attached workers. The shaded bar indicates a period of business recession as defined by the National Bureau of Economic Research.
SOURCE: Department of Labor, Bureau of Labor Statistics.

rate holding steady, the employment-to-population ratio climbed noticeably higher in 2014 and early 2015 after having moved more or less sideways for much of the recovery. The quit rate, which is often perceived as a measure of worker confidence in labor market opportunities, has largely recovered to its pre-recession level. Moreover, an index constructed by Federal Reserve Board staff that aims to summarize movements in a wide array of labor market indicators also suggests that labor market conditions strengthened further in 2014, and that the gains have been quite strong in recent months (figure 4).[1]

. . . while gains in compensation have been modest . . .

Even as the labor market has been improving, most measures of labor compensation have continued to show only modest gains. The employment cost index (ECI) for private industry workers, which measures both wages and the cost of employer-provided benefits, rose 2¼ percent over the 12 months ending in December, only slightly faster than the gains of about 2 percent that had prevailed for several years. Two other prominent measures of compensation—average hourly earnings and business-sector compensation per hour—increased slightly less than the ECI over the past year and have shown fewer signs of acceleration (figure 5). Over the past five years, the gains in all three of these measures of nominal compensation have fallen well short of their pre-recession averages and have only slightly outpaced inflation. That said, the drop in energy prices has pushed up real wages in recent months.

4. Change in labor market conditions index

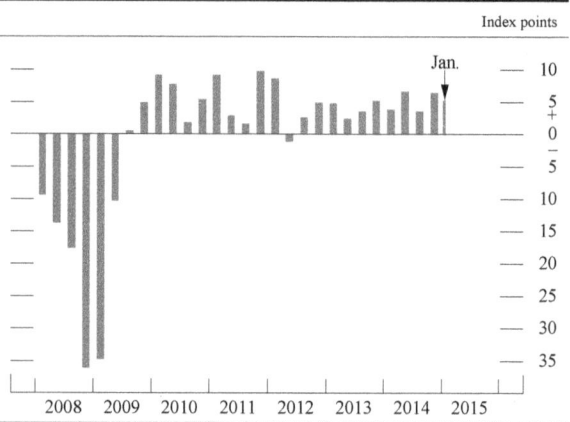

NOTE: The index has a mean of zero and a standard deviation of 100; an increase indicates an improvement in labor market conditions. Quarterly figures are averages of monthly changes.

SOURCE: Federal Reserve Board staff estimates based on data from the Conference Board; Department of Labor, Bureau of Labor Statistics and Employment and Training Administration; National Federation of Independent Business.

5. Measures of change in hourly compensation

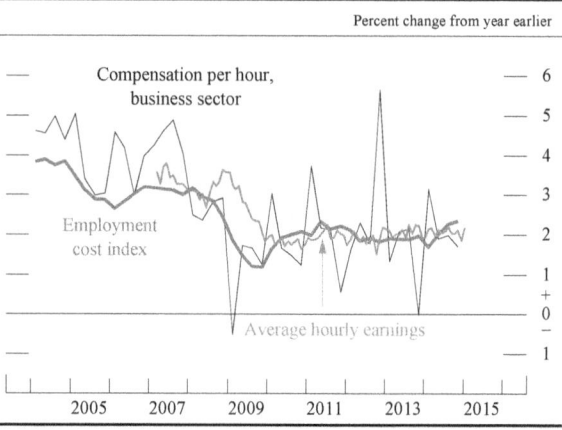

NOTE: The average hourly earnings data series begins in March 2007 and extends through January 2015. The compensation per hour and employment cost index data extend through 2014:Q4. For business-sector compensation, change is over four quarters; for the employment cost index, change is over the 12 months ending in the last month of each quarter; for average hourly earnings, change is from 12 months earlier.

SOURCE: Department of Labor, Bureau of Labor Statistics.

---

1. For details on the construction of the labor market conditions index, see Hess Chung, Bruce Fallick, Christopher Nekarda, and David Ratner (2014), "Assessing the Change in Labor Market Conditions," Finance and Economics Discussion Series 2014-109 (Washington: Board of Governors of the Federal Reserve System, December), www.federalreserve.gov/econresdata/feds/2014/files/2014109pap.pdf.

6. Change in total business sector output per hour

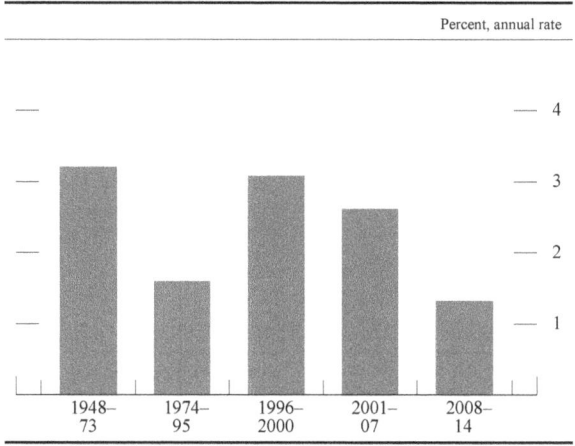

Percent, annual rate

NOTE: Changes are measured from Q4 of the year immediately preceding the period through Q4 of the final year of the period.
SOURCE: Department of Labor, Bureau of Labor Statistics.

... and productivity growth has been lackluster

Over time, increases in productivity are the central determinant of improvements in living standards. Labor productivity in the private business sector has increased at an average annual pace of 1¼ percent since the recession began in late 2007. This pace is close to the average that prevailed between the mid-1970s and the mid-1990s, but it is well below the pace of the earlier post–World War II period and the period from the mid-1990s to the eve of the financial crisis (figure 6). In recent years, productivity growth has been held down by, among other factors, the sharp drop in businesses' capital expenditures over the recession and the moderate recovery in expenditures since then. Productivity gains may be better supported in the future as investment continues to strengthen.

A plunge in crude oil prices has held down consumer prices ...

As discussed in the box "The Effect of the Recent Decline in Oil Prices on Economic Activity," crude oil prices have plummeted since June 2014. This sharp drop has caused overall consumer price inflation to slow, mainly due to falling gasoline prices: The national average of retail gasoline prices moved down from about $3.75 per gallon in June to about $2.20 per gallon in January. Crude oil prices have turned slightly higher in recent weeks, and futures markets suggest that prices are expected to edge up further in coming years; nevertheless, oil prices are still expected to remain well below the levels that had prevailed through last June.

Over the past six months, increases in food prices have moderated. Consumer food price increases had been somewhat elevated in early 2014 as a result of rising food commodity prices, but those commodity prices have since eased, and increases at the retail level have slowed accordingly.

. . . but even outside of the energy and food categories, inflation has remained subdued

Inflation for items other than food and energy (so-called core inflation) remains modest. Core PCE prices rose at an annual rate of only about 1 percent over the last six months of 2014 after having risen at a 1¾ percent rate in the first half of the year; for 2014 as a whole, core PCE prices were up a little more than 1¼ percent (figure 7). The trimmed mean PCE price index, an alternative indicator of underlying inflation constructed by the Federal Reserve Bank of Dallas, also increased more slowly in the second half of last year. Falling import prices likely held down core inflation in the second half of the year; lower oil prices, and easing prices for commodities more generally, may have played a role as well. In addition, ongoing resource slack has reinforced the low-inflation environment, though with the improving economy, downward pressure from this factor is likely waning.

Looking at the overall basket of items that people consume, price increases remain muted and below the FOMC's longer-run objective of 2 percent. In December, the PCE price index was only ¾ percent above its level from a year earlier. With retail surveys showing a further sharp decline in gasoline prices in January, overall consumer prices likely moved lower early this year.

Survey-based measures of longer-term inflation expectations have remained stable, while market-based measures of inflation compensation have declined

The Federal Reserve tracks indicators of inflation expectations because such expectations likely factor into wage- and price-setting decisions and so influence actual inflation. Survey-based measures of longer-term inflation expectations, including surveys of both households and professional

7. Change in the chain-type price index for personal consumption expenditures

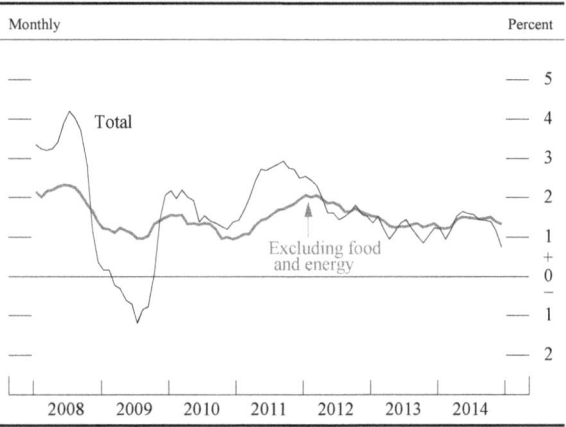

NOTE: The data extend through December 2014; changes are from one year earlier.
SOURCE: Department of Commerce, Bureau of Economic Analysis.

The Effect of the Recent Decline in Oil Prices on Economic Activity

Since June, the price of crude oil has fallen sharply, on net, with the spot price of Brent (the blue line in figure A) dropping about 50 percent and the price of the December 2017 futures contract (the black line in figure A) declining about 25 percent. Although weaker-than-expected global oil demand has contributed to the fall in prices, much of the decline is likely due to favorable supply factors, including the rapid growth of U.S. oil production, the surprising strength of oil exports from Libya and Iraq, and OPEC's decision to maintain production levels despite declining prices. The drop in oil prices has a number of economic implications, including a sizable but temporary reduction in consumer price inflation. This discussion reviews some of the channels through which the recent fall in oil prices is anticipated to affect economic activity in the United States and globally.

One important channel through which a decline in oil prices affects the global economy is the transfer of wealth from oil producers to oil consumers. As shown in the table, the largest net oil-importing

countries—and thus the prime beneficiaries of lower oil prices—are the emerging Asian economies, Japan, the euro area, and, despite recent sharp increases in oil production, the United States.[1] Losses are concentrated in the oil-producing countries, including those of the Middle East, Russia, Venezuela, and, to a lesser extent, Canada and Mexico. (Lower oil prices have also destabilized financial markets in Russia and Venezuela.) Globally, the wealth transfer nets to zero, but the overall

---

1. Although many of the largest oil importers also are oil producers, and thus have some domestic losses as well as gains, net exports of oil by country provides a useful proxy for the global distribution of gains and losses following a price change.

A. Brent spot and futures prices

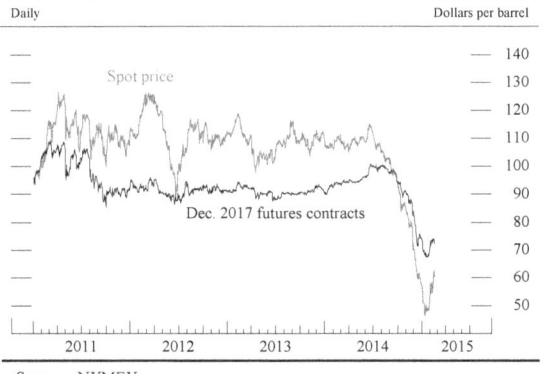

Daily   Dollars per barrel

Spot price

Dec. 2017 futures contracts

2011   2012   2013   2014   2015

SOURCE: NYMEX.

Net oil and petroleum product exports

	Millions of barrels per day	Percent of GDP
Emerging Asia ex. China	−9.9	−5.9
Japan	−4.4	−3.7
Euro area	−9.2	−3.0
China	−5.8	−2.6
United States	−6.6	−1.6
Central and South America ex. Venezuela	−0.8	−0.8
Mexico	0.9	2.8
Canada	1.6	3.7
Russia	7.0	13.8
Middle East	19.1	29.8
Venezuela	1.7	31.0

NOTE: The data are for 2013. Share of GDP is an approximation based on net export volumes valued at the Brent price on June 17, 2014 ($113.30). GDP is gross domestic product.
SOURCE: Department of Energy; International Monetary Fund.

effect on global economic activity is likely to be stimulative in the near term; oil consumers tend to spend a substantial portion of the windfall, while oil producers generally absorb at least some of the initial effect through reduced saving or higher borrowing.

In the United States, the wealth transfer just discussed is likely to be most apparent in supporting consumer spending, as lower gasoline prices boost the real disposable income of consumers. Indeed, the recent rise in consumer sentiment and improvements in survey measures of expected income growth suggest that households are reacting quite positively to lower gasoline prices.

The stimulus from higher U.S. consumption is likely to be somewhat offset by reduced investment in the oil sector. Already there has been a sharp decline in the number of oil drilling rigs in operation (figure B), and a number of oil companies have cut their capital expenditure plans. Nonetheless, the direct effect on U.S. gross domestic product (GDP)

of such a decline will be small because investment in the oil sector—though rising in recent years—accounts for only about 1 percent of GDP.

Lower oil-sector investment is likely to weigh on U.S. oil production, which has grown at a torrid pace in recent years (figure C). So far, however, U.S. oil production has yet to decline. The continued strength of production despite falling investment reflects both a propensity to cut investment in the least productive projects first and a large stock of partially completed wells that are likely to still come on line.

While there is a general consensus that lower oil prices should boost U.S. and global economic activity, considerable uncertainty exists regarding the ultimate size of the effect. All in all, however, for the United States as a whole, it is likely that the additional disposable income resulting from lower gasoline prices will provide a significant boost to consumer spending that will far exceed the drag from lower investment in the oil sector.

B. Domestic oil drilling rigs in operation

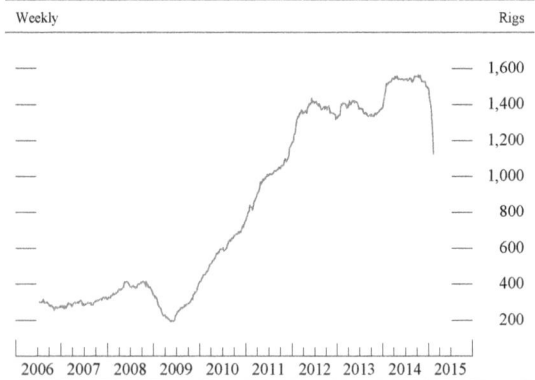

NOTE: The data, which are seasonally adjusted by Board staff, extend through February 13, 2015.
SOURCE: Baker Hughes Company.

C. Domestic crude oil extraction

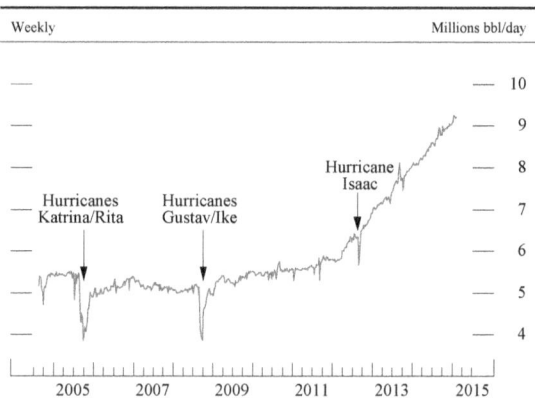

NOTE: The data, which are seasonally adjusted by Board staff, extend through February 13, 2015. Bbl is barrels of oil.
SOURCE: Department of Energy, U.S. Energy Information Administration.

8.   Median inflation expectations

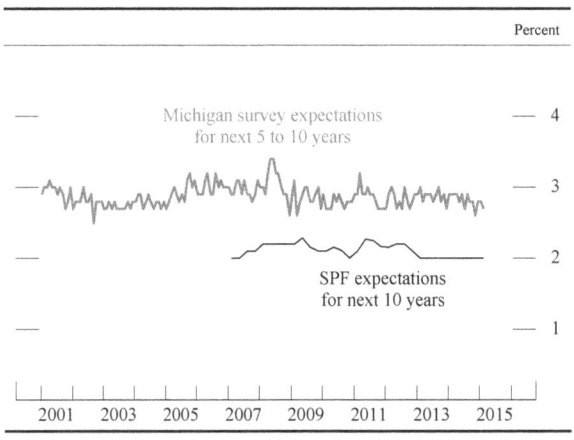

NOTE: The Michigan survey data are monthly and extend through February 2015. The SPF data for inflation expectations for personal consumption expenditures are quarterly and extend from 2007:Q1 through 2015:Q1.
SOURCE: University of Michigan Surveys of Consumers; Survey of Professional Forecasters (SPF).

9.   Change in real gross domestic product, gross domestic income, and private domestic final purchases

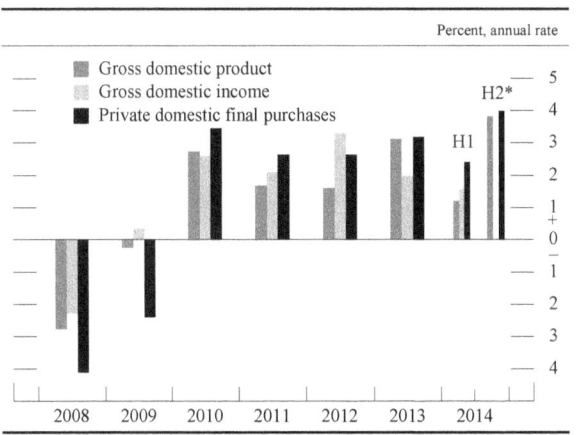

* Gross domestic income is not yet available for 2014:H2.
SOURCE: Department of Commerce, Bureau of Economic Analysis.

forecasters, have been quite stable over the past 15 years; in particular, they have changed little, on net, over the past few years (figure 8). In contrast, measures of longer-term inflation compensation derived from financial market instruments have fallen noticeably during the past several months. As is discussed in more detail in the box "Challenges in Interpreting Measures of Longer-Term Inflation Expectations," deducing the sources of changes in inflation compensation is difficult because such movements may be caused by factors other than shifts in market participants' inflation expectations.

Economic activity expanded at a strong pace in the second half of 2014

Real GDP is estimated to have increased at an annual rate of 3¾ percent in the second half of last year after a reported increase of just 1¼ percent in the first half, when output was likely restrained by severe weather and other transitory factors (figure 9). Private domestic final purchases—a measure of household and business spending that tends to exhibit less quarterly variation than GDP—also advanced at a substantial pace in the second half of last year.

The second-half gains in GDP reflected solid advances in consumer spending and in business investment spending on equipment and intangibles (E&I) as well as subdued gains for both residential investment and nonresidential structures. More generally, the growth in GDP has been supported by accommodative financial conditions, including declines in the cost of borrowing for many households and businesses; by a reduction in the restraint from fiscal policy relative to 2013; and by increases in spending spurred by continuing job gains and, more recently, by falling oil prices. The gains in GDP have occurred despite an appreciating U.S. dollar and concerns about global economic growth, which remain an important source of uncertainty for the economic outlook.

Consumer spending was supported by continuing improvement in the labor market and falling oil prices, . . .

Real PCE rose at an annual rate of 3¾ percent in the second half of 2014—a noticeable step-up from the sluggish rate of only about 2 percent in the first half (figure 10). The increases in spending have been supported by the improving labor market. In addition, the fall in gasoline and other energy prices has boosted purchasing power for consumers, especially those in lower- and middle-income brackets who spend a sizable share of their income on gasoline. Real disposable personal income—that is, income after taxes and adjusted for price changes—rose 3 percent at an annual rate in the second half of last year, roughly double the average rate recorded over the preceding five years.

. . . further increases in household wealth and low interest rates, . . .

Consumer spending growth was also likely supported by further increases in household net worth, as the stock market continued to rise and house prices moved up in the second half of last year. The value of corporate equities rose about 10 percent in 2014, on top of the 30 percent gain seen in 2013. Although the gains in house prices slowed last year—for example, the CoreLogic national index increased only 5 percent after having risen more substantially in 2012 and 2013— these gains affected a larger share of the population than did the gains in equities, as more individuals own homes than own stocks (figure 11). Reflecting increases in home and equity prices, aggregate household net wealth has risen appreciably from its levels during the recession and its aftermath to more than

10. Change in real personal consumption expenditures and disposable personal income

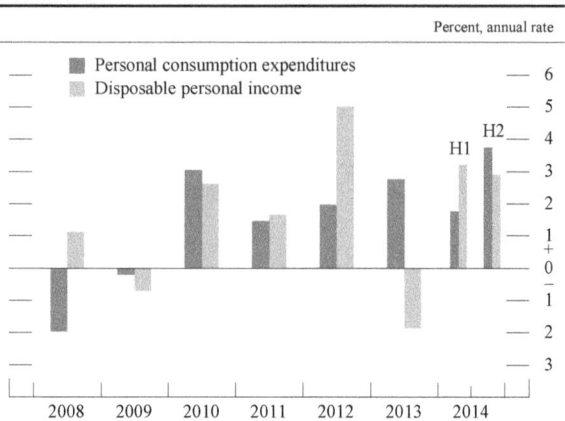

SOURCE: Department of Commerce, Bureau of Economic Analysis.

11. Prices of existing single-family houses

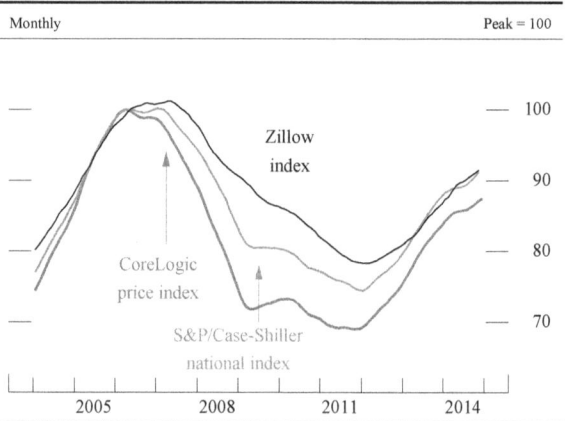

NOTE: The data for the Zillow and S&P/Case-Shiller indexes extend through November 2014. The data for the CoreLogic index extend through December 2014. Each index has been normalized so that its peak is 100. The CoreLogic price index includes purchase transactions only and is adjusted by Federal Reserve Board staff. The S&P/Case-Shiller index reflects all arm's-length sales transactions nationwide.
SOURCE: The S&P/Case-Shiller U.S. National Home Price Index ("Index") is a product of S&P Dow Jones Indices LLC and/or its affiliates and has been licensed for use by the Board. Copyright © 2015 S&P Dow Jones Indices LLC, a subsidiary of the McGraw Hill Financial Inc., and/or its affiliates. All rights reserved. Redistribution, reproduction and/or photocopying in whole or in part are prohibited without written permission of S&P Dow Jones Indices LLC. For more information on any of S&P Dow Jones Indices LLC's indices please visit www.spdji.com. S&P® is a registered trademark of Standard & Poor's Financial Services LLC and Dow Jones® is a registered trademark of Dow Jones Trademark Holdings LLC. Neither S&P Dow Jones Indices LLC, Dow Jones Trademark Holdings LLC, their affiliates nor their third party licensors make any representation or warranty, express or implied, as to the ability of any index to accurately represent the asset class or market sector that it purports to represent and neither S&P Dow Jones Indices LLC, Dow Jones Trademark Holdings LLC, their affiliates nor their third party licensors shall have any liability for any errors, omissions, or interruptions of any index or the data included therein.

Challenges in Interpreting Measures of Longer-Term Inflation Expectations

In many economic models, inflation expectations are an important determinant of the behavior of actual inflation. For this reason, measures of inflation expectations are widely followed. Although none of the available measures is perfect, surveys of individuals, economists, and professional forecasters all shed some light on the inflation expectations of different groups. For the most part, these survey-based measures have been quite stable in recent years in the United States. Many analysts credit that stability with helping to keep the variation in actual inflation fairly limited despite pressures (such as the deep recession and sharp changes in energy prices) that might have had the potential to induce more substantial and long-lasting changes in inflation.

Measures of expected inflation can also be derived from financial instruments whose payouts are linked to inflation. For example, inflation compensation implied by Treasury Inflation-Protected Securities (TIPS), known as the TIPS breakeven inflation rate, is defined as the difference, at comparable maturities, between yields on nominal Treasury securities and yields on TIPS, which are indexed to headline consumer price index (CPI) inflation. Inflation swaps—contracts in which one party makes payments of certain fixed nominal amounts in exchange for cash flows that are indexed to cumulative CPI inflation over some horizon—provide alternative measures of inflation compensation. These measures of inflation compensation provide information about market participants' expectations of inflation, but that information is generally obscured by other sources of variation.

Both of those market-based measures of inflation compensation have declined noticeably since early August (figure A). Focusing on inflation compensation 5 to 10 years ahead is useful, particularly for monetary policy, because it gives a sense of where market participants expect inflation to settle in the long term after developments influencing inflation in the short term have run their course. The 5-to-10-year-forward inflation compensation measure computed from TIPS fell from an annual rate of around 2½ percent in early August to below 2 percent in January; over the same period, the swaps-based measure fell from around 2¾ percent to a little more than 2 percent. Market participants have offered several potential explanations for these declines, including the effects of the plunge in

oil prices and soft readings on overall and core inflation as well as concerns about the global growth outlook and disinflationary pressure abroad.[1]

The Federal Open Market Committee's (FOMC) 2 percent inflation objective is stated in terms of the price index for personal consumption expenditures (PCE), and PCE price inflation tends to run a few tenths of a percentage point lower, on average, than the CPI inflation used in pricing TIPS and inflation swaps. Thus, if these recent readings on inflation compensation could be interpreted as direct measures of expected CPI inflation, then they would probably correspond to expectations for PCE inflation that are lower than the Committee's objective. Recent FOMC statements have noted that the Committee will monitor both survey measures and these market-based inflation compensation measures closely.

---

1. In support of the latter explanation, market participants also noted the decline of inflation compensation abroad, in particular in the euro area. One possible reason for the effects of oil prices and realized inflation on longer-term inflation compensation is that, in response to changes in the intermediate-term inflation outlook, investors are reportedly more likely to adjust their positions in the more recently issued, and thus more liquid, longer-term TIPS rather than the older-vintage TIPS with shorter remaining maturities.

A.   5-to-10-year-forward inflation compensation

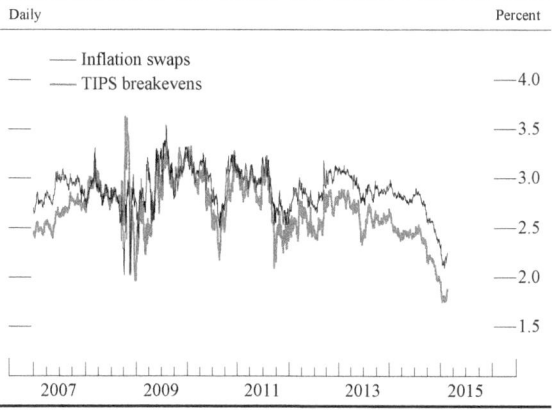

NOTE: TIPS is Treasury Inflation-Protected Securities.
SOURCE: Federal Reserve Bank of New York; Barclays; Federal Reserve Board staff estimates.

Inflation compensation is distinct from inflation expectations, however, as both TIPS- and swaps-based measures of inflation compensation reflect not only expected inflation, but also an inflation risk premium—the compensation that holders of nominal securities demand for bearing inflation risk—as well as other premiums driven by liquidity differences and shifts in the relative supply and demand of nominal versus inflation-indexed securities. Federal Reserve System staff maintain several term structure models aimed at disentangling the various components of inflation compensation and providing estimates of inflation expectations and risk premiums.[2] Most staff models suggest that 5-to-10-year inflation expectations have remained relatively stable since last summer. Instead, the models tend to attribute at least part of the decline in inflation compensation to some reduction in inflation risk premiums and the effects of the other factors included in the models. However, these models cannot fully explain the recent decline in inflation compensation.

Distributions of future inflation derived from surveys and inflation options also display an interesting divergence. Distributions of inflation 5 to 10 years ahead that are derived from surveys of primary dealers

have remained stable since last summer—consistent with the stability of the other survey measures cited earlier. In contrast, information gleaned from 10-year inflation options (that is, caps and floors, which pay the holder when inflation is higher or lower than specified levels) suggests that investors may have recently become more concerned about lower inflation outcomes and less concerned about higher inflation outcomes. This shift could reflect an increase in the investors' perceived likelihood of low inflation outcomes, but it could also reflect an increased willingness to pay higher premiums for insurance against such outcomes as well as other possible factors depressing long-horizon inflation compensation.

Thus, the results from the Federal Reserve's staff models are consistent with readings from surveys of primary dealers, economists, professional forecasters, and consumers, all of which indicate that longer-run inflation expectations have remained generally stable (figure B). However, given the uncertainties in inferring inflation expectations from the market measures of inflation compensation, one cannot rule out a decline in inflation expectations among market participants.

2. For further details, see Michael Abrahams, Tobias Adrian, Richard Crump, and Emanuel Moench (2012), "Decomposing Real and Nominal Yield Curves," Federal Reserve Bank of New York Staff Reports, no. 570 (New York: FRB New York, September, revised October 2013), www.newyorkfed.org/research/staff_reports/sr570.html; Jens H.E. Christensen, Jose A. Lopez, and Glenn D. Rudebusch (2010), "Inflation Expectations and Risk Premiums in Arbitrage-Free Model of Nominal and Real Bond Yields," *Journal of Money, Credit and Banking*, vol. 42 (September, issue supplement s1), pp. 143–78; Stefania D'Amico, Don H. Kim, and Min Wei (2014), "Tips from TIPS: The Informational Content of Treasury Inflation-Protected Security Prices," Finance and Economics Discussion Series 2014-24 (Washington: Board of Governors of the Federal Reserve System, January), www.federalreserve.gov/pubs/feds/2014/201424/201424pap.pdf; Andrea Ajello, Luca Benzoni, and Olena Chyruk (2012), "Core and 'Crust': Consumer Prices and the Term Structure of Interest Rates," available at SSRN: http://ssrn.com/abstract=1851906 or http://dx.doi.org/10.2139/ssrn.1851906; and Joseph G. Haubrich, George G. Pennacchi, and Peter Ritchken (2012), "Inflation Expectations, Real Rates, and Risk Premia: Evidence from Inflation Swaps," *Review of Financial Studies*, vol. 25 (5), pp. 1588–629.

B. Survey measures of longer-term inflation expectations

NOTE: The Survey of Professional Forecasters (SPF) series starts on March 2007 and extends through March 2015. The Blue Chip consensus series starts on June 2007 and extends through December 2014. The Survey of Primary Dealers series starts on January 2011 and extends through January 2015. CPI is consumer price index.

SOURCE: Federal Reserve Bank of Philadelphia, Survey of Professional Forecasters (SPF); Blue Chip Financial Forecasts; Federal Reserve Bank of New York, Survey of Primary Dealers.

12.   Wealth-to-income ratio

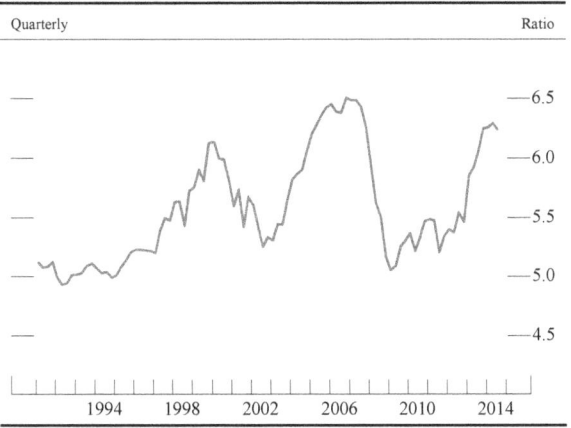

NOTE: The data extend through 2014:Q3. The series is the ratio of household net worth to disposable personal income.
SOURCE: For net worth, Federal Reserve Board, Statistical Release Z.1, "Financial Accounts of the United States"; for income, Department of Commerce, Bureau of Economic Analysis.

13.   Household debt service

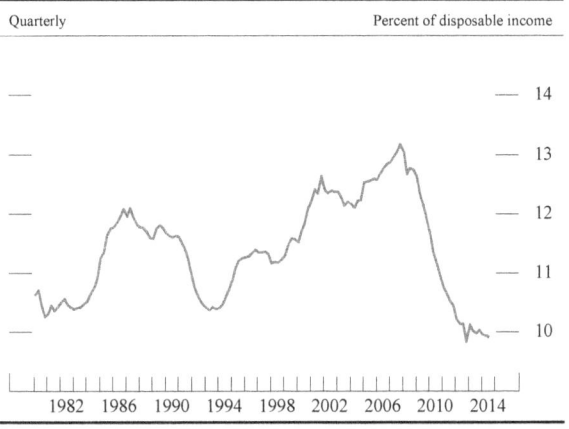

NOTE: The data extend through 2014:Q3. Debt service payments consist of estimated required payments on outstanding mortgage and consumer debt.
SOURCE: Federal Reserve Board, Statistical Release, "Household Debt Service and Financial Obligations Ratios."

14.   Changes in household debt

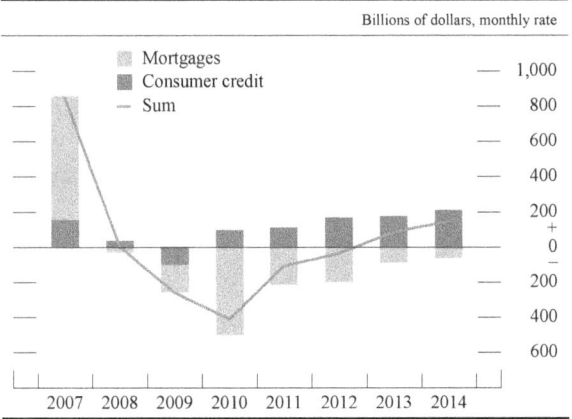

NOTE: Changes are calculated from year-end to year-end, except 2014 changes, which are calculated from Q3 to Q3.
SOURCE: Federal Reserve Board, Statistical Release Z.1, "Financial Accounts of the United States."

six times the value of disposable personal income (figure 12).

Coupled with low interest rates, the rise in incomes has lowered debt payment burdens for many households. The household debt service ratio—that is, the ratio of required principal and interest payments on outstanding household debt to disposable personal income—has remained at a very low level by historical standards (figure 13).

. . . and increased credit availability for consumers

Consumer credit continued to expand through late 2014, as auto and student loans have remained available even to borrowers with lower credit scores (figure 14). In addition, credit cards have become somewhat more accessible to individuals on the lower end of the credit spectrum, and overall credit card debt increased moderately last year.

Consumer confidence has moved up

Consistent with the improvement in the labor market and the fall in energy prices, indicators of consumer sentiment moved up noticeably in the second half of last year. The University of Michigan Surveys of Consumers' index of consumer sentiment—which incorporates households' views about their own financial situations as well as broader economic conditions—has moved up strongly, on net, in recent months and is now close to its long-run average (figure 15). The Michigan survey's measure of households' expectations of real income changes in the year ahead has also continued to trend up over the past several months, perhaps reflecting the fall in gasoline prices. However, this measure remains substantially below its historical average and suggests a more guarded outlook than the headline sentiment index.

However, the pace of homebuilding has improved only slowly

After advancing reasonably well in 2012 and early 2013, the recovery in residential construction activity has slowed markedly. Single-family housing starts only edged up in 2014, and multifamily construction activity was also little changed (figure 16). And sales of both new and existing homes were flat, on net, last year (figure 17). In all, real residential investment rose only 2½ percent in 2014, and it remains well below its pre-recession peak. The weak recovery in construction likely relates to the rate of household formation, which, notwithstanding tentative signs of a recent pickup, has generally stayed very low despite the improvement in the labor market.

Lending policies for home purchases remained tight overall, although there are some indications that mortgage credit has started to become more widely accessible. Over the course of 2014, the fraction of home-purchase mortgages issued to borrowers with credit scores on the lower end of the spectrum edged up. Additionally, in the Senior Loan Officer Opinion Survey on Bank Lending Practices (SLOOS), several large banks reported having eased lending standards on prime home-purchase loans in the third and fourth quarters of last year.[2] In January, the Federal Housing Administration reduced its mortgage insurance premiums by about one-third of the level that had prevailed during the past four years—a step that may lower the cost of credit for households with small down payments and low credit scores. Even so, mortgages have remained difficult to obtain for many households.

Meanwhile, for borrowers who can qualify for a mortgage, the cost of credit is low. After rising appreciably around mid-2013, mortgage interest rates have since retraced much of those increases. The 30-year fixed mortgage rate declined roughly 60 basis points in 2014, and it has edged down further, on net, this year to a level not far from its all-time low

---

2. The SLOOS is available on the Board's website at www.federalreserve.gov/boarddocs/snloansurvey.

15.   Indexes of consumer sentiment and income expectations

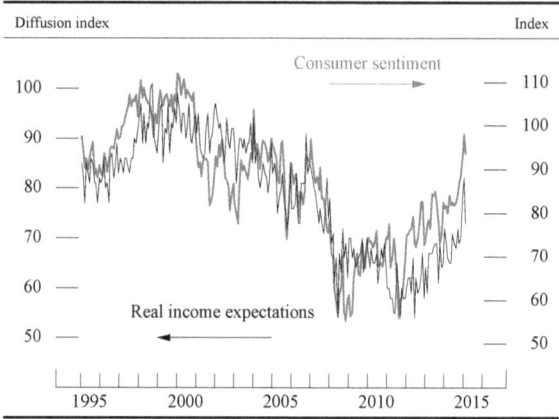

NOTE: The data are monthly and extend through February 2015. Consumer sentiment is indexed to 100 in 1966. Real income expectations are calculated as the net percent of survey respondents expecting family income to go up more than prices during the next year or two.
SOURCE: University of Michigan Surveys of Consumers.

16.   Private housing starts and permits

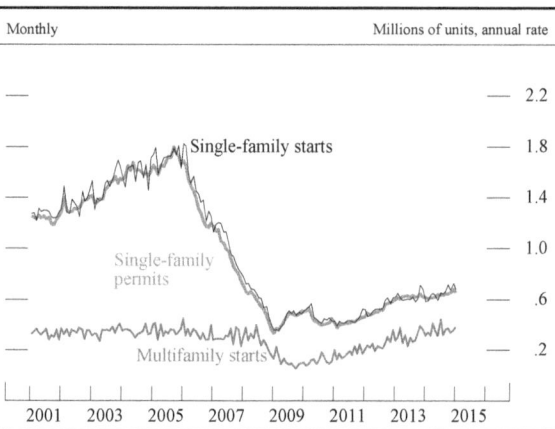

SOURCE: Department of Commerce, Bureau of the Census.

17.   New and existing home sales

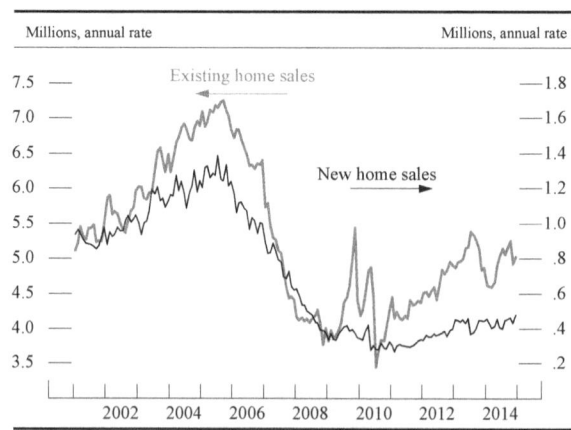

NOTE: The data extend through December 2014. "Existing home sales" includes single-family, condo, townhome, and co-op sales.
SOURCE: For new single-family home sales, Census Bureau; for existing home sales, National Association of Realtors.

18.   Mortgage interest rate and mortgage refinance index

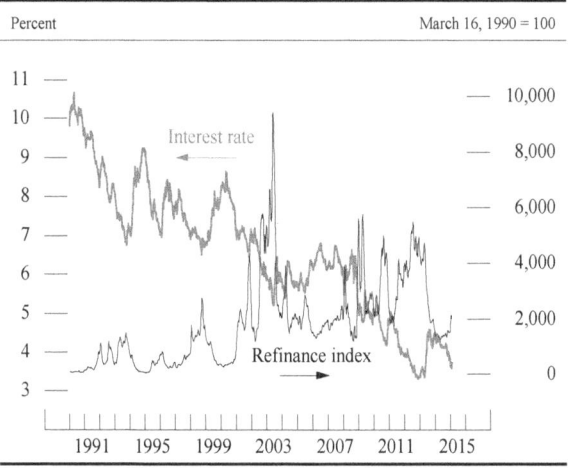

NOTE: The interest rate data are for 30-year fixed-rate mortgages and are weekly through February 18, 2015. The refinance index data are a seasonally adjusted 4-week moving average through February 13, 2015.
SOURCE: For interest rate data, Freddie Mac Primary Mortgage Market Survey, from Freddie Mac (Federal Home Loan Mortgage Corporation), www.freddiemac.com/pmms; for refinance index data, the Mortgage Bankers Association.

19.   Change in real business fixed investment

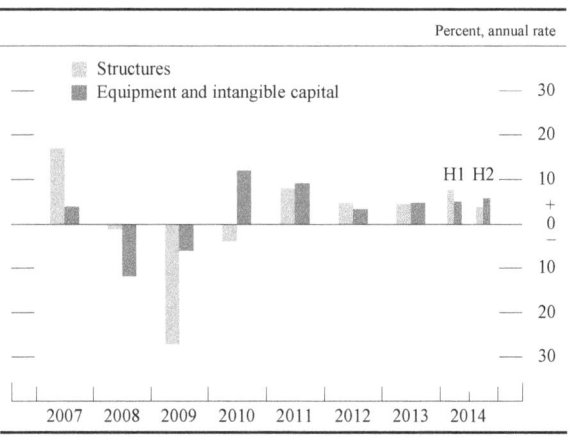

SOURCE: Department of Commerce, Bureau of Economic Analysis.

20.   Selected components of net financing for nonfinancial businesses

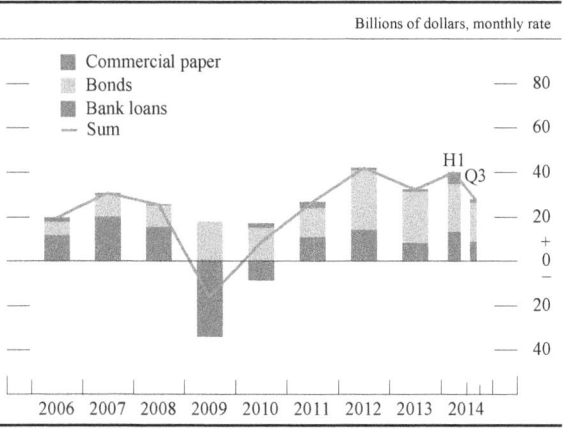

NOTE: The data for the components except bonds are seasonally adjusted.
SOURCE: Federal Reserve Board, Statistical Release Z.1, "Financial Accounts of the United States."

in 2012 (figure 18). Likely related to the most recent decline in mortgage rates, refinancing activity rose modestly in January.

Overall business investment has moved up, but investment in the energy sector is starting to be affected by the drop in oil prices

Business fixed investment rose at an annual rate of 5¼ percent in the second half of 2014, close to the rate of increase seen in the first half. Spending on E&I capital rose at an annual rate of about 6 percent, while spending on nonresidential structures moved up about 4 percent (figure 19). Business investment has been supported by strengthening final demand as well as by low interest rates and generally accommodative financial conditions. Regarding nonresidential structures, vacancy rates for existing properties have been declining, and financing conditions for new construction have eased further—both factors that bode well for future construction. More recently, however, the steep decline in the number of drilling rigs in operation suggests that a sharp falloff in the drilling and mining component of investment in nonresidential structures may be under way.

Corporate financing conditions were generally favorable

The financial condition of large nonfinancial firms generally remained solid in the second half of last year; profitability stayed high, and default rates on nonfinancial corporate bonds were generally very low. Nonfinancial firms have continued to raise funds through capital markets at a robust pace, given sturdy corporate credit quality, historically low interest rates on corporate bonds, and highly accommodative lending conditions for most firms (figures 20 and 21). Bond issuance by investment-grade nonfinancial firms, and syndicated lending to those firms, have both been particularly strong. However, speculative-grade issuance in those markets, which had remained elevated for most of 2014, diminished late in the year, because volatility increased and spreads widened and perhaps also because of greater scrutiny by regulators of syndicated leveraged loans with weaker credit quality and lower repayment capacity.

Credit also was readily available to most bank-dependent businesses. According to the October 2014 and January 2015 SLOOS reports, banks generally continued to ease price and nonprice terms on commercial and industrial (C&I) loans to firms of all sizes in the second half of 2014. That said, in the fourth quarter, several banks reported having tightened lending policies for oil and gas firms or, more broadly, in response to legislative, supervisory, or accounting changes. In addition, although overall C&I loans on banks' books registered substantial increases in the second half of 2014, loans to businesses in amounts of $1 million or less—a proxy for lending to small businesses—increased only modestly. The weak growth in these small loans appears largely due to sluggish demand; however, bank lending standards to small businesses are still reportedly somewhat tighter than the midpoint of their range over the past decade despite considerable loosening over the past few years.

Net exports held down second-half real GDP growth slightly

Exports increased at a modest pace in the second half of 2014, held back by lackluster growth abroad as well as the appreciation of the dollar. Import growth was also relatively subdued, despite the impetus from the stronger dollar, and was well below the pace observed in the first half (figure 22). All told, real net trade was a slight drag on real GDP growth in the second half of 2014.

The current account deficit was little changed in the third quarter of 2014 and, at 2¼ percent of nominal GDP, was near its narrowest reading since the late 1990s (figure 23). The current account deficit in the first three quarters of 2014 was financed mainly by purchases of Treasury and corporate securities

21. Corporate bond yields, by securities rating

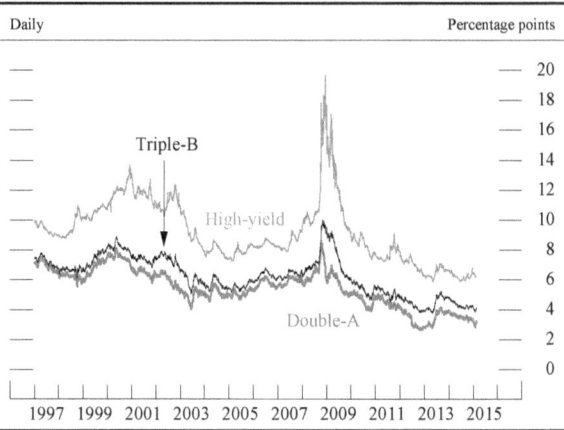

NOTE: The yields shown are yields on 10-year bonds.
SOURCE: BofA Merrill Lynch Global Research, used with permission.

22. Change in real imports and exports of goods and services

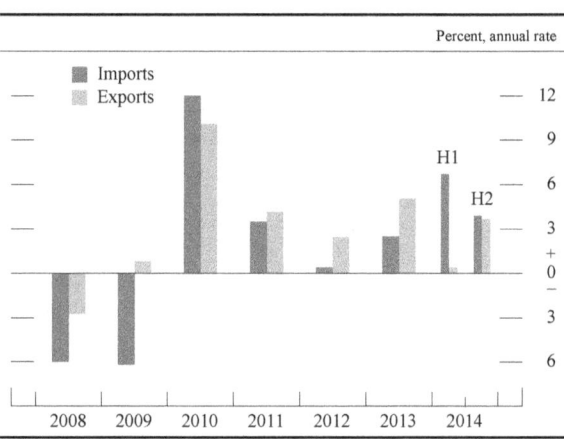

SOURCE: Department of Commerce, Bureau of Economic Analysis.

23. U.S. trade and current account balances

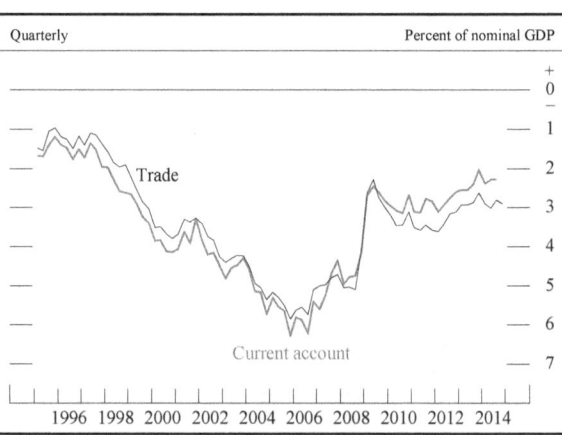

NOTE: The data for the current account extend through 2014:Q3. GDP is gross domestic product.
SOURCE: Department of Commerce, Bureau of Economic Analysis.

24. U.S. net financial inflows

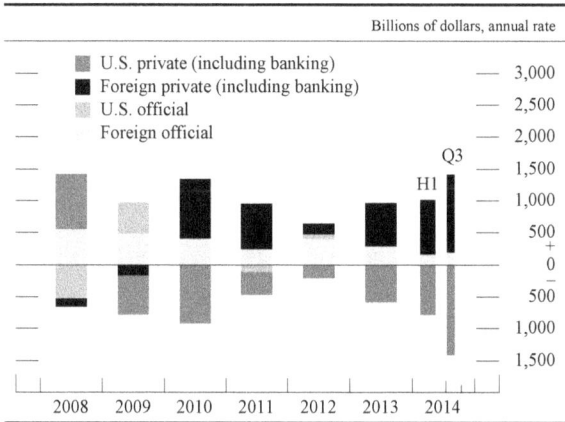

NOTE: Negative numbers indicate a balance of payments outflow, generated when U.S. residents, on net, purchase foreign assets or when foreign residents, on net, sell U.S. assets. A negative number for "U.S. private" or "U.S. official" indicates an increase in U.S. residents' holdings of foreign assets. U.S. official flows include the foreign currency acquired when foreign central banks draw on their swap lines with the Federal Reserve.
SOURCE: Department of Commerce, Bureau of Economic Analysis.

25. Change in real government expenditures on consumption and investment

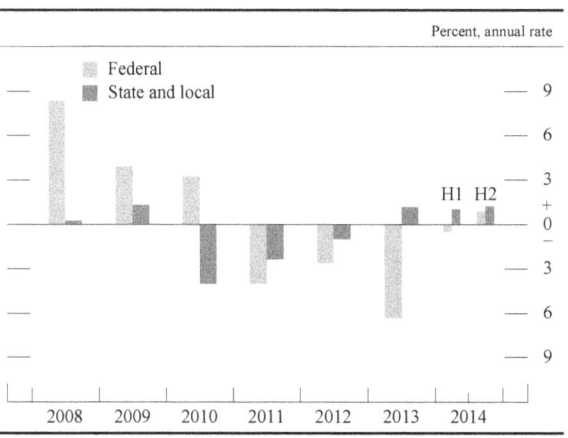

SOURCE: Department of Commerce, Bureau of Economic Analysis.

by foreign private investors (figure 24). In contrast, the pace of foreign official purchases in the first three quarters of the year was the slowest in more than a decade, reflecting a significant slowdown in reserve accumulation by emerging market economies (EMEs).

Federal fiscal policy was less of a drag on GDP . . .

Fiscal policy at the federal level had been a factor restraining GDP growth for several years, especially in 2013. In 2014, however, the contractionary effects of tax and spending changes eased appreciably as the restraining effects of the 2013 tax increases abated and there was a slowing in the declines in federal purchases due to sequestration and the Budget Control Act of 2011 (figure 25). Moreover, some of the overall drag on demand was offset in 2014 by an increase in transfers resulting from the Affordable Care Act.

The federal unified deficit narrowed further last year, reflecting both the previous years' spending cuts and an increase in tax receipts resulting from the ongoing economic expansion (figure 26). The budget deficit was 2¾ percent of GDP for fiscal year 2014, and the Congressional Budget Office projects that it will be about 2½ percent in 2015. As a result, overall federal debt held by the public stabilized as a share of GDP in 2014, albeit at a relatively high level (figure 27).

. . . and state and local government expenditures are also turning up

The expansion of economic activity has also led to continued slow improvements in the fiscal position of most state and local governments. Consistent with improving finances, states and localities expanded employment rolls in 2014 (figure 28). Furthermore, state and local expenditures on construction projects rose a touch last year following several years of declines.

Financial Developments

The expected path for the federal funds rate flattened

Market participants seemed to judge the incoming domestic economic data since the middle of last year, especially the employment reports, as supporting expectations for continued economic expansion in the United States; however, concerns about the foreign economic outlook weighed on investor sentiment. On balance, market-based measures of the expected (or mean) path of the federal funds rate through late 2017 have flattened, but the expected timing of the initial increase in the federal funds rate from its current target range was about unchanged. In addition, according to the results of the most recent Survey of Primary Dealers and the Survey of Market Participants, both conducted by the Federal Reserve Bank of New York just prior to the January FOMC meeting, respondents judged that the initial increase in the target federal funds rate was most likely to occur around mid-2015, little changed from the results of those surveys from last June.[3] Meanwhile, in part because the passage of time brought the anticipated date of the initial increase in the federal funds rate closer, measures of policy rate uncertainty based on interest rate derivatives edged higher, on net, from their mid-2014 levels.

Longer-term Treasury yields and other sovereign benchmark yields declined

Yields on longer-term Treasury securities have continued to move down since the middle of last year on net (figure 29). In particular, the yields on 10- and 30-year nominal Treasury securities declined about 40 basis points and 60 basis points, respectively, from their levels at the end of June 2014. The decreases in

3. The results of the Survey of Primary Dealers and of the Survey of Market Participants are available on the Federal Reserve Bank of New York's website at www.newyorkfed.org/markets/primarydealer_survey_questions.html and www.newyorkfed.org/markets/survey_market_participants.html, respectively.

26. Federal receipts and expenditures

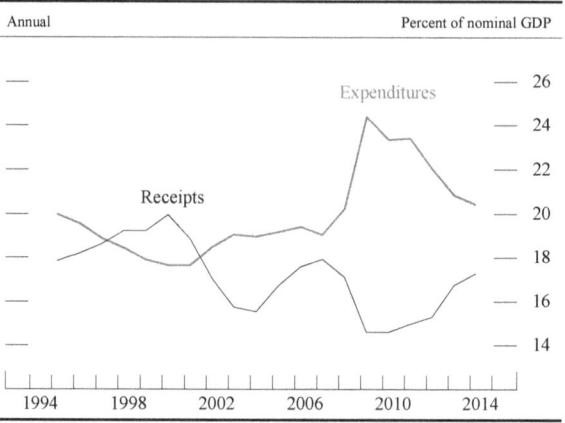

NOTE: The receipts and expenditures data are on a unified-budget basis and are for fiscal years (October through September); gross domestic product (GDP) data are for the four quarters ending in Q3.
SOURCE: Office of Management and Budget.

27. Federal government debt held by the public

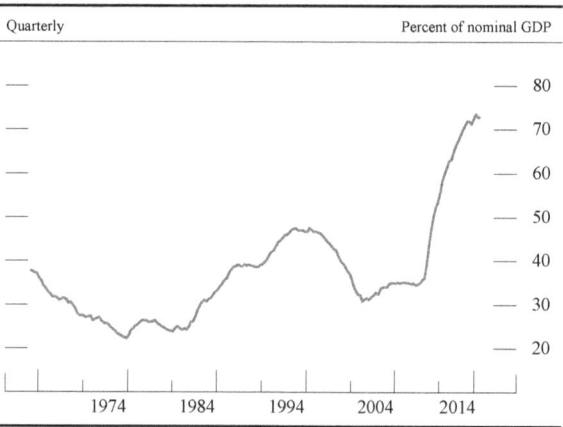

NOTE: The data extend through 2014:Q3. The data for gross domestic product (GDP) are at an annual rate. Debt held by the public is debt held at the end of the period.
SOURCE: Department of Commerce, Bureau of Economic Analysis; Department of the Treasury, Bureau of the Fiscal Service.

28. State and local government employment change

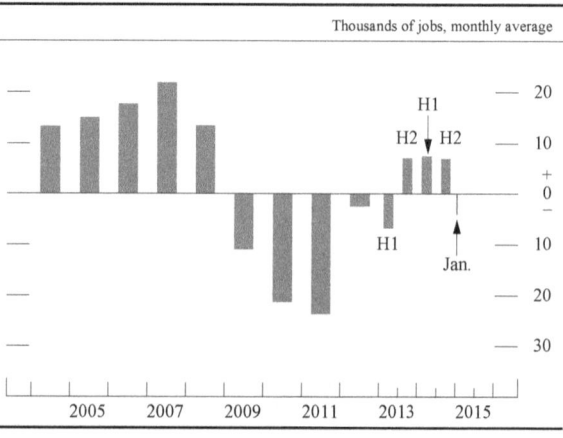

SOURCE: Department of Labor, Bureau of Labor Statistics.

29. Yields on nominal Treasury securities

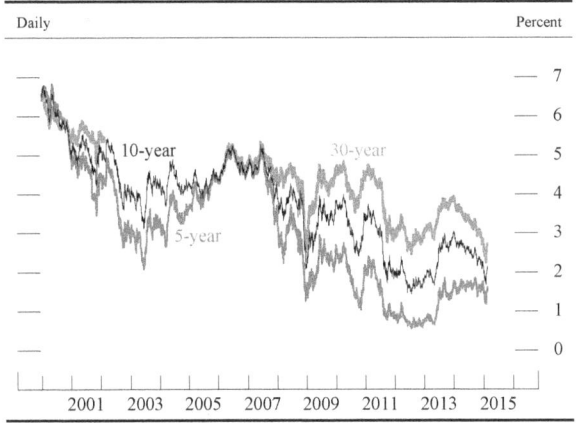

Daily   Percent

NOTE: The Treasury ceased publication of the 30-year constant maturity series on February 18, 2002, and resumed that series on February 9, 2006.
SOURCE: Department of the Treasury.

longer-term yields were driven especially by reductions in longer-horizon forward rates. For example, the 5-year forward rate 5 years ahead dropped about 80 basis points over the same period. Long-term benchmark sovereign yields in advanced foreign economies (AFEs) have also moved down significantly in response to disappointing growth and very low and declining rates of inflation in a number of foreign countries as well as the associated actual and anticipated changes in monetary policy abroad.

The declines in longer-term Treasury yields and long-horizon forward rates seem to largely reflect reductions in term premiums—the extra return investors expect to obtain from holding longer-term securities as opposed to holding and rolling over a sequence of short-term securities for the same period. Market participants pointed to several factors that may help to explain the reduction in term premiums. First, very low and declining AFE yields and safe-haven flows associated with the deterioration in the foreign economic outlook likely have increased demand for Treasury securities. Second, the weaker foreign economic outlook coupled with the steep decline in oil prices may have led investors to put higher odds on scenarios in which U.S. inflation remains quite low for an extended period. Investors may see nominal long-term Treasury securities as an especially good hedge against such risks. Finally, market participants may have increased the probability they attach to outcomes in which U.S. economic growth is persistently subdued. Indeed, the 5-year forward real yield 5 years ahead, obtained from yields on Treasury Inflation-Protected Securities, has declined further, on net, since the middle of last year and stands well below levels commonly cited as estimates of the longer-run real short rate.

Consistent with moves in the yields on longer-term Treasury securities, yields on 30-year agency mortgage-backed securities (MBS)—an important determinant of mortgage interest rates—decreased about 30 basis points, on balance, over the second half of 2014 and early 2015 (figure 30).

Liquidity conditions in Treasury and agency MBS markets were generally stable . . .

On balance, indicators of Treasury market functioning remained stable over the second half of 2014 even as the Federal Reserve trimmed the pace of its asset purchases and ultimately brought the purchase program to a close at the end of October. The Treasury market experienced a sharp drop in yields and significantly elevated volatility on October 15, as technical factors reportedly amplified price movements following the release of the somewhat weaker-than-expected September U.S. retail sales data. However, market conditions recovered quickly and liquidity measures, such as bid-asked spreads, have been generally stable since then. Moreover, Treasury auctions generally continued to be well received by investors.

As in the Treasury market, liquidity conditions in the agency MBS market were generally stable, with the exception of mid-October. Dollar-roll-implied financing rates for production coupon MBS—an indicator of the scarcity of agency MBS for settlement— suggested limited settlement pressures in these markets over the second half of 2014 and early 2015 (figure 31).

. . . and short-term funding markets also continued to function well as rates moved slightly higher overall

Conditions in short-term dollar funding markets also remained stable during the second half of 2014 and early 2015. Both unsecured and secured money market rates moved modestly higher late in 2014 but remained close to their averages since the federal funds rate reached its effective lower bound. Unsecured offshore dollar funding markets generally did not exhibit signs of

30. Yield and spread on agency mortgage-backed securities

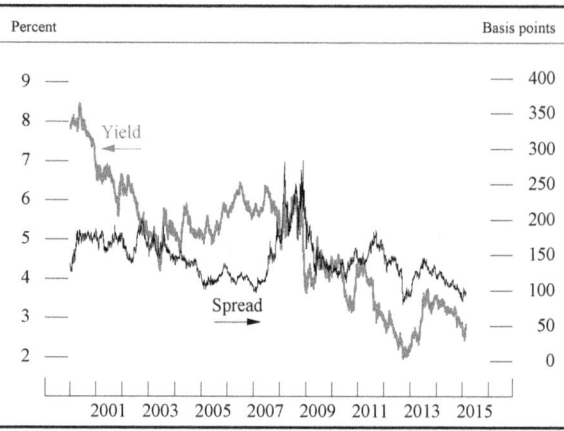

NOTE: The data are daily. Yield shown is for the Fannie Mae 30-year current coupon, the coupon rate at which new mortgage-backed securities would be priced at par, or face, value. Spread shown is to the average of the 5- and 10-year nominal Treasury yields.
SOURCE: Department of the Treasury; Barclays.

31. Dollar-roll-implied financing rates (front month), Fannie Mae 30-year current coupon

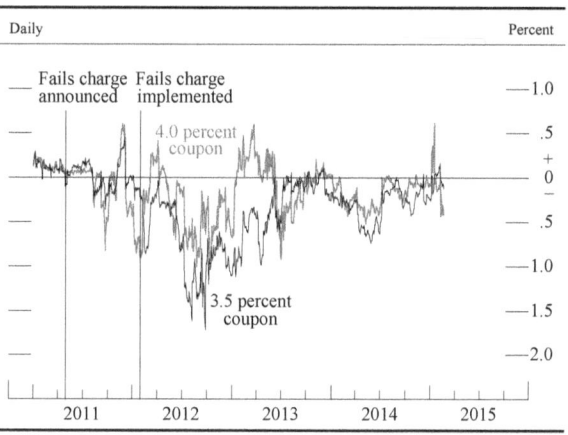

SOURCE: J.P. Morgan.

stress, and the repurchase agreement, or repo, market functioned smoothly with modest year-end pressures.

Money market participants continued to focus on the ongoing testing of the Federal Reserve's monetary policy tools. The offering rate in the overnight reverse repurchase agreement (ON RRP) exercise has continued to provide a soft floor for other rates on secured borrowing, and the term RRP testing operations that were conducted in December and matured in early January seemed to help alleviate year-end pressures in money markets. For a detailed discussion of the testing of monetary policy tools, see the box "Additional Testing of Monetary Policy Tools" in Part 2.

Broad equity price indexes rose despite higher volatility, while risk spreads on corporate debt widened

Over the second half of 2014 and early 2015, broad measures of U.S. equity prices increased further, on balance, but stock prices for the energy sector declined substantially, reflecting the sharp drops in oil prices (figure 32). Although increased concerns about the foreign economic outlook seemed to weigh on risk sentiment, the generally positive tone of U.S. economic data releases as well as declining longer-term interest rates appeared to provide support for equity prices. Overall equity valuations by some conventional measures are somewhat higher than their historical average levels, and valuation metrics in some sectors continue to appear stretched relative to historical norms. Implied volatility for the S&P 500 index, as calculated from options prices, increased moderately, on net, from low levels over the summer.

Corporate credit spreads, particularly those for speculative-grade bonds, widened from the fairly low levels of last summer, in part because of the underperformance of energy firms. Overall, corporate bond spreads across the credit spectrum have been near their historical median levels recently. For further

32.   Equity prices

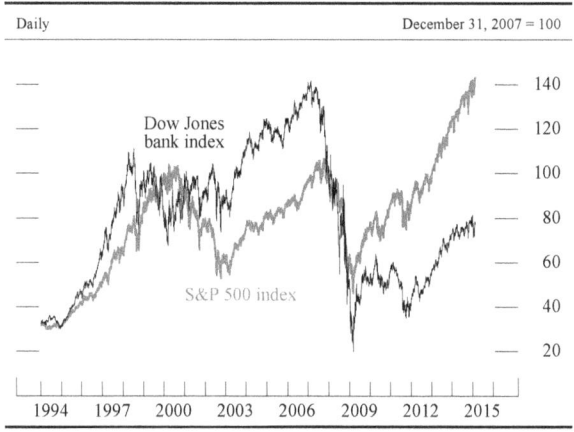

Daily   December 31, 2007 = 100

Dow Jones bank index

S&P 500 index

140
120
100
80
60
40
20

1994   1997   2000   2003   2006   2009   2012   2015

SOURCE: Dow Jones bank index and Standard & Poor's 500 index via Bloomberg.

discussion of asset prices and other financial stability issues, see the box "Developments Related to Financial Stability."

Bank credit and the M2 measure of the money stock continued to expand

Aggregate credit provided by commercial banks increased at a solid pace in the second half of 2014 (figure 33). The expansion in bank credit was mainly driven by moderate loan growth coupled with continued robust expansion of banks' holdings of U.S. Treasury securities, which was reportedly influenced by efforts of large banks to meet the new Basel III Liquidity Coverage Ratio requirements. The growth of loans on banks' books was generally consistent with the SLOOS reports of increased loan demand and further easing of lending standards for many loan categories over the second half of 2014. Meanwhile, delinquency and charge-off rates fell across most major loan types.

Measures of bank profitability were little changed in the second half of 2014, on net, and remained below their historical averages (figure 34). Equity prices of large domestic bank holding companies (BHCs) have increased moderately, on net, since the middle of last year (figure 32). Credit default swap (CDS) spreads for large BHCs were about unchanged.

The M2 measure of the money stock has increased at an average annualized rate of about 5½ percent since last June, below the pace registered in the first half of 2014 and about in line with the pace of nominal GDP. The deceleration was driven by a moderation in the growth rate of liquid deposits in the banking sector relative to the first half of 2014. Although demand for currency weakened in the third quarter of 2014 relative to the first half of the year, currency growth has been strong since November.

33. Ratio of total commercial bank credit to nominal gross domestic product

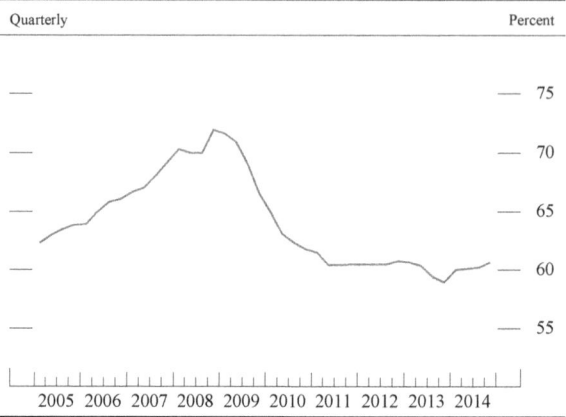

SOURCE: Federal Reserve Board, Statistical Release H.8, "Assets and Liabilities of Commercial Banks in the United States"; Department of Commerce, Bureau of Economic Analysis.

34. Profitability of bank holding companies

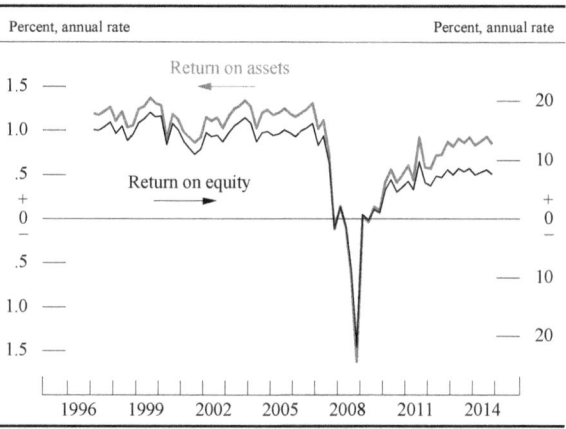

NOTE: The data, which are seasonally adjusted, are quarterly.
SOURCE: Federal Reserve Board, FR Y-9C, Consolidated Financial Statements for Bank Holding Companies.

Developments Related to Financial Stability

The financial vulnerabilities in the U.S. financial system overall have remained moderate since the previous *Monetary Policy Report*. In the past few years, capital and liquidity positions in the banking sector have continued to improve, net wholesale short-term funding in the financial sector has decreased substantially, and aggregate leverage of the private nonfinancial sector has not picked up. However, valuation pressures are notable in some asset markets, although they have eased a little on balance. Leverage at lower-rated nonfinancial firms has become more pronounced. Recent developments in Greece have rekindled concerns about the country defaulting and exiting the euro system.

With regard to asset valuations, price-to-earnings and price-to-sales ratios are somewhat elevated, suggesting some valuation pressures. However, estimates of the equity premium remain relatively wide, as the long-run expected return on equity exceeds the low real Treasury yield by a notable margin, suggesting that investors still expect somewhat higher-than-average compensation relative to historical standards for bearing the additional risk associated with holding equities. Risk spreads for corporate bonds have widened over recent months, especially for speculative-grade firms, in part because of concerns about the credit quality of energy-related firms, though yields remain near historical lows, reflecting low term premiums. Residential real estate valuations appear within historical norms, with recent data pointing to some cooling of house price gains in regions that recently experienced rapid price appreciation. However, valuation pressures in the commercial real estate market may have increased in recent quarters as prices have risen relative to rents, and underwriting standards in securitizations have weakened somewhat, though debt growth remains moderate.

The private nonfinancial sector credit-to-GDP ratio has declined to roughly its level in the mid-2000s. At lower-rated and unrated nonfinancial businesses, however, leverage has continued to increase with the rapid growth in high-yield bond issuance and leveraged loans in recent years. The underwriting quality of leveraged loans arranged or held by banking institutions in 2014:Q4 appears to have improved slightly, perhaps in response to the stepped-up enforcement of the leveraged lending guidance. However, new deals continue to show signs of weak underwriting terms and heightened leverage that are close to levels preceding the financial crisis.

As a result of steady improvements in capital and liquidity positions since the financial crisis, U.S. banking firms, in aggregate, appear to be better positioned to absorb potential shocks—such as those related to litigation, falling oil prices, and financial contagion originating abroad—and to meet strengthening credit demand. The sharp decline in oil prices, if sustained, may lead to credit strains for some banks with concentrated exposures to the energy sector, but at banks that are more diversified, potential losses are likely to be offset by the positive effects of lower oil prices on the broader economy. Thirty-one large bank holding companies (BHCs) are currently undergoing their annual stress tests, the results of which are scheduled to be released in March.

Leverage in the nonbank financial sector appears, on balance, to be at moderate levels. New securitizations, which contribute to financial sector leverage, have been boosted by issuance of commercial mortgage-backed securities (CMBS) and collateralized loan obligations (CLOs), which remained robust amid continued reports of relatively accommodative underwriting standards for the underlying assets. That said, the risk retention rules finalized in October, which require issuers to retain at least 5 percent of any securitizations issued, have the potential to affect market activity, especially in the private-label residential mortgage-backed securities, non-agency CMBS, and CLO sectors.

Reliance on wholesale short-term funding by nonbank financial institutions has declined significantly in recent years and is low by historical standards. However, prime money market funds with a fixed net asset value remain vulnerable to investor runs if there is a fall in the market value of their assets. Furthermore, the growth of bond mutual funds and exchange-traded funds (ETFs) in recent years means that these funds now hold a much higher fraction of the available stock of relatively less liquid assets—such as high-yield corporate debt, bank loans, and international debt—than they did before the financial crisis. As mutual funds and ETFs may appear to offer greater liquidity than the markets in which they transact, their growth heightens the potential for a forced sale in the underlying markets if some event were to trigger large volumes of redemptions.

Since the previous *Monetary Policy Report*, the Federal Reserve has taken further steps to improve the resiliency of the financial system. First, the Federal Reserve Board and other federal banking agencies finalized several rules to enhance the capital and liquidity positions of large banking organizations. In particular, a final rule on a liquidity coverage ratio was issued, requiring large and internationally active banking organizations to hold a certain minimum amount of high-quality liquid assets, such as central bank reserves and government and corporate debt that can be converted easily and quickly into cash. Another final rule was adopted to modify the definition of the supplementary leverage ratio in a manner consistent with the recent changes agreed to by the Basel Committee on Banking Supervision. The technical modifications adjust the amount of certain off-balance-sheet items included in the ratio, such as credit derivatives, repurchase agreement–style transactions, and lines of credit. The changes strengthen the ratio by more appropriately capturing a banking organization's on- and off-balance-sheet exposures and, based on estimates, would increase capital requirements, on balance, across banking firms.

In addition, the Federal Reserve issued several rules to conform to Dodd-Frank Act mandates. A final rule was issued to implement section 622 of the act, which generally prohibits a financial company (defined generally as an insured depository institution or depository institution holding company) from combining with another company if the resulting company's liabilities would exceed 10 percent of the aggregate consolidated liabilities of all such financial companies. Another final rule, issued jointly by several federal agencies, requires the sponsors of asset-backed securities (ABS) to retain not less than 5 percent of the credit risk of the assets collateralizing the ABS issuance unless certain underwriting criteria on the securitized assets are met. The rule also generally prohibits the sponsor from transferring or hedging that credit risk. Moreover, several federal agencies jointly issued a proposed rule establishing minimum margin requirements for certain swap contracts that are not cleared through central counterparties.

In addition, the Federal Reserve proposed a rule to further strengthen the capital positions of the most systemically important U.S. bank holding companies (BHCs). The proposal establishes a methodology to identify whether a U.S. BHC is a global systemically important banking organization (GSIB) and so would be subject to a risk-based capital surcharge calibrated based on its systemic profile. A GSIB would be required to calculate its capital surcharge under two methods and would be subject to the higher of the two surcharges. The first method is consistent with the Basel frame work, which results in capital surcharges ranging from 1.0 to 2.5 percent. The second method, which takes into account a measure of the firm's' reliance on short-term wholesale funding, results in capital surcharges ranging from 1.0 to 4.5 percent. Failure to maintain the capital surcharge would subject the GSIB to restrictions on capital distributions and discretionary bonus payments.

Finally, the Federal Reserve invited public comment on enhanced prudential standards for the regulation and supervision of General Electric Capital Corporation (GECC), a nonbank financial company that the Financial Stability Oversight Council has designated for supervision by the Federal Reserve Board. In light of the substantial similarity of GECC's activities and risk profile to those of a similarly sized BHC, the Federal Reserve is proposing to apply enhanced prudential standards to GECC similar to those applied to large BHCs.

Municipal bond markets functioned smoothly, but some issuers remained strained

Credit conditions in municipal bond markets have generally remained stable since the middle of last year. Over that period, the MCDX—an index of CDS spreads for a broad portfolio of municipal bonds—and ratios of yields on 20-year general obligation municipal bonds to those on longer-term Treasury securities increased slightly.

Nevertheless, significant financial strains were still evident for some issuers. Puerto Rico, with speculative-grade-rated general obligation bonds, continued to face challenges from subdued economic performance, severe indebtedness, and other fiscal pressures. Meanwhile, the City of Detroit emerged from bankruptcy late in 2014 after its debt restructuring plan was approved by a federal judge.

International Developments

Bond yields in the advanced foreign economies continued to decline . . .

As noted previously, long-term sovereign yields in the AFEs moved down further during the second half of 2014 and into early 2015 on continued low inflation readings abroad and heightened concerns over the strength of foreign economic growth as well as amid substantial monetary policy accommodation (figure 35). German yields fell to record lows, as the European Central Bank (ECB) implemented new liquidity facilities, purchased covered bonds and asset-backed securities, and announced it would begin buying euro-area sovereign bonds. Specifically, the ECB said that it would purchase €60 billion per month of euro-area public and private bonds through at least September 2016. Japanese yields also declined, reflecting the expansion by the Bank of Japan (BOJ) of its asset purchase program. In the United Kingdom, yields fell as data showed declining inflation and some moderation in economic growth, although they

35. 10-year nominal benchmark yields in advanced foreign economies

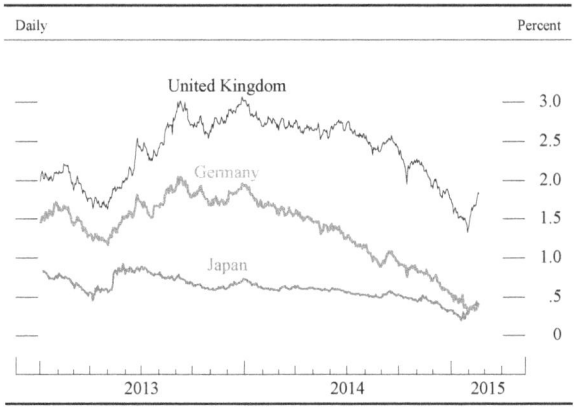

SOURCE: Bloomberg.

have retraced a little of that move in recent weeks, in part as market sentiment toward the U.K. outlook appears to have improved somewhat. In emerging markets, yields were mixed—falling, for the most part, in Asia and generally rising modestly in Latin America—as CDS spreads widened amid growing credit concerns, particularly in some oil-exporting countries.

. . . while the dollar has strengthened markedly

The broad nominal value of the dollar has increased markedly since the middle of 2014, with the U.S. dollar appreciating against almost all currencies (figure 36). The increase in the value of the dollar was largely driven by additional monetary easing abroad and rising concerns about foreign growth—forces similar to those that drove benchmark yields lower—in the face of expectations of solid U.S. growth and the anticipated start of monetary tightening in the United States later this year. Both the euro and the yen have depreciated about 20 percent against the dollar since mid-2014. Notwithstanding the sharp nominal appreciation of the dollar since mid-2014, the real value of the dollar, measured against a broad basket of currencies, is currently somewhat below its historical average since 1973 and well below the peak it reached in early 1985 (figure 37).

Foreign equity indexes were mixed over the period (figure 38). Japanese equities outperformed other AFE indexes, helped by the BOJ's asset purchase expansion. Euro-area equities are up modestly from their mid-2014 levels, boosted recently by monetary easing. However, euro-area bank shares substantially underperformed broader indexes, partly reflecting low profitability, weak operating environments, and lingering vulnerabilities to economic and financial shocks. EME equities indexes were mixed, with most emerging Asian indexes rising and some of the major Latin American indexes moving down.

36.   U.S. dollar exchange rate against broad index and selected major currencies

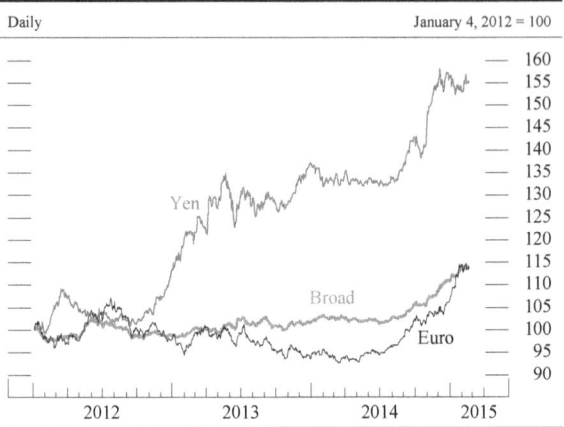

NOTE: The data are in foreign currency units per dollar.
SOURCE: Federal Reserve Board, Statistical Release H.10, "Foreign Exchange Rates."

37.   Broad real value of the dollar

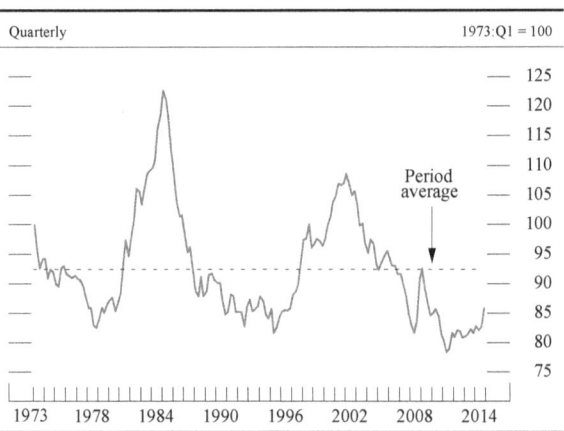

NOTE: The data are in foreign currency units per dollar.
SOURCE: Federal Reserve Board, Statistical Release H.10, "Foreign Exchange Rates."

38.   Equity indexes for selected foreign economies

SOURCE: For emerging markets, Morgan Stanley Emerging Markets MXEF Capital Index; for the euro area, Dow Jones Euro STOXX Index; for Japan, Tokyo Stock Price Index (TOPIX).

39. Real gross domestic product growth in selected
     advanced foreign economies

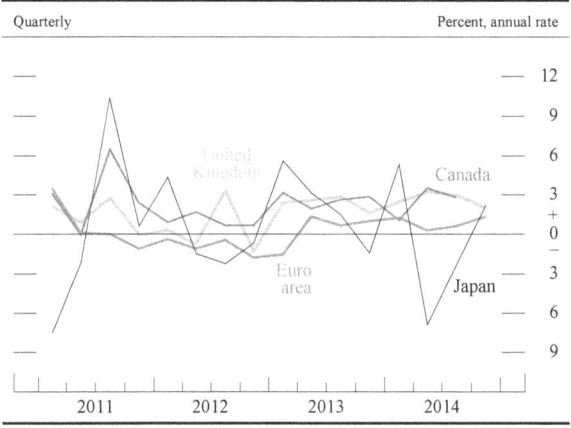

Quarterly	Percent, annual rate

NOTE: The data for Canada extend through 2014:Q3. The data for the United Kingdom, the euro area, and Japan extend through 2014:Q4.
SOURCE: For Canada, Statistics Canada; for the United Kingdom, Office for National Statistics; for the euro area, Eurostat; for Japan, Cabinet Office, Government of Japan.

Economic growth in the advanced foreign economies, while still generally weak, firmed toward the end of the year

Economic growth in the AFEs, which was weak in the first half of 2014, firmed toward the end of the second half of the year, supported in part by lower oil prices and more accommodative monetary policies (figure 39). The euro-area economy barely grew in the third quarter and unemployment remained near record highs, but the pace of economic activity moved up in the fourth quarter. Notwithstanding more supportive monetary policy and the recent pickup in euro-area growth, negotiations over additional financial assistance for Greece have the potential to trigger adverse market reactions and resurrect financial stresses that might impair growth in the broader euro-area economy. Japanese real GDP contracted again in the third quarter, following a tax hike–induced plunge in the second quarter, but it rebounded toward the end of the year as exports and household spending increased. In contrast, economic activity in the United Kingdom and Canada was robust in the third quarter but moderated in the fourth quarter.

The fall in oil prices and other commodity prices pushed down headline inflation across the major AFEs. Most notably, 12-month euro-area inflation continued to trend down, falling to negative 0.6 percent in January. Declines in inflation and in market-based measures of inflation expectations since mid-2014 prompted the ECB to increase its monetary stimulus. Similar considerations led the BOJ to step up its pace of asset purchases in October. The Bank of Canada lowered its target for the overnight rate in January in light of the depressing effect of lower oil prices on Canadian inflation and economic activity, as oil exports are nearly 20 percent of total goods exports. Several other foreign central banks lowered their policy rates, either reaching or pushing further into negative territory, including in Denmark, Sweden, and

Switzerland—the last of which did so in the context of removing its floor on the euro-Swiss franc exchange rate.

Growth in the emerging market economies improved but remained subdued

Following weak growth earlier last year, overall economic activity in the EMEs improved a bit in the second half of 2014, but performance varied across economies. Growth in Asia was generally solid, supported by external demand, particularly from the United States, and improved terms of trade due to the sharp decline in commodity prices. In contrast, the decline in commodity prices, along with macroeconomic policy challenges, weighed on economic activity in several South American countries.

In China, exports expanded rapidly in the second half of last year, but fixed investment softened, as real estate investment slowed amid a weakening property market. Responding to increased concerns over the strength of growth, the authorities announced additional targeted stimulus measures in an effort to prevent the economy from slowing abruptly. In much of the rest of emerging Asia, exports, particularly to the United States, supported a step-up in growth from the first half of the year. The Mexican economy continued to grow at a moderate pace in the second half of 2014, with solid exports to the United States but lingering softness in household demand. In Brazil, economic activity remained lackluster amid falling commodity prices, diminished business confidence, and tighter macroeconomic policy. Declining oil prices were especially disruptive for several economies with heavy dependence on oil exports, including Russia and Venezuela.

Inflation continued to be subdued in most EMEs. The fall in the price of oil contributed to a moderation of headline inflation in several EMEs, including China. However, this contribution was limited in many EMEs due to the prevalence of administered energy prices, which lower the pass-through of changes in oil prices to consumer prices. In several countries, including Indonesia and Malaysia, the fall in energy prices prompted governments to cut fuel subsidies, leading to a rise in domestic prices of fuel and in inflation late in 2014. With inflation low or declining, some central banks, including those of China, Korea, and Chile, loosened monetary policy to support growth. In other EMEs, including Brazil and Malaysia, inflationary pressures stemming from depreciating currencies or from reductions in fuel subsidies prompted central banks to raise policy rates. The central bank of Russia sharply tightened monetary policy to combat inflationary pressures and stabilize its financial markets, which came under considerable pressure in late 2014.

PART 2
MONETARY POLICY

The Federal Open Market Committee (FOMC) concluded its asset purchase program at the end of October in light of the substantial improvement in the outlook for the labor market since the inception of the program. To support further progress toward maximum employment and price stability, the FOMC has kept the target federal funds rate at its effective lower bound and maintained the Federal Reserve's holdings of longer-term securities at sizable levels. To give greater clarity to the public about its policy outlook, the Committee has also continued to provide qualitative guidance regarding the future path of the federal funds rate. In particular, the Committee indicated at its two most recent meetings that it can be patient in beginning to normalize the stance of monetary policy and continued to emphasize the data-dependent nature of its policy stance. Following its September meeting, and as part of prudent planning, the Committee announced updated principles and plans for the eventual normalization of monetary policy.

The FOMC concluded its asset purchases at the end of October in light of substantial improvement in the outlook for the labor market

At the end of October, the FOMC ended the asset purchase program that began in September 2012 after having made further measured reductions in the pace of its asset purchases at the prior meetings in July and September.[4] The decision to end the purchase program reflected the substantial improvement in the outlook for the labor market since the program's inception—which had been the goal of the asset purchases—and the Committee's judgment that the overall recovery was sufficiently strong to support ongoing progress toward the Committee's policy objectives. However, the Committee judged that a high degree of policy accommodation still remained appropriate and maintained its existing policy of reinvesting principal payments from its holdings of agency debt and agency mortgage-backed securities (MBS) in agency MBS and of rolling over maturing Treasury securities at auction. By keeping the Federal Reserve's holdings of longer-term securities at sizable levels, this policy is expected to help maintain accommodative financial conditions by putting

downward pressure on longer-term interest rates and supporting mortgage markets. In turn, those effects are expected to contribute to progress toward both the maximum employment and price stability objectives of the FOMC.

To support further progress toward its objectives, the Committee has kept the target federal funds rate at its lower bound and updated its forward rate guidance

The Committee has maintained the exceptionally low target range of 0 to ¼ percent for the federal funds rate to support further progress toward its objectives of maximum employment and price stability (figure 40). In addition, the FOMC has provided guidance about the likely future path of the federal funds rate in an effort to give greater clarity to the public about its policy outlook. In particular, the Committee has reiterated that, in determining how long to maintain this target range, it will assess realized and expected progress toward its objectives. This assessment will continue to take into account a wide range of information, including measures of labor market conditions, indicators of inflation pressures and inflation expectations, and readings on financial and international developments. Based on its assessment of these factors, before updating its guidance in December, the Committee had been indicating that it likely would be appropriate to maintain

---

4. See Board of Governors of the Federal Reserve System (2014), "Federal Reserve Issues FOMC Statement," press release, October 29, www.federalreserve.gov/newsevents/press/monetary/20141029a.htm.

40.   Selected interest rates

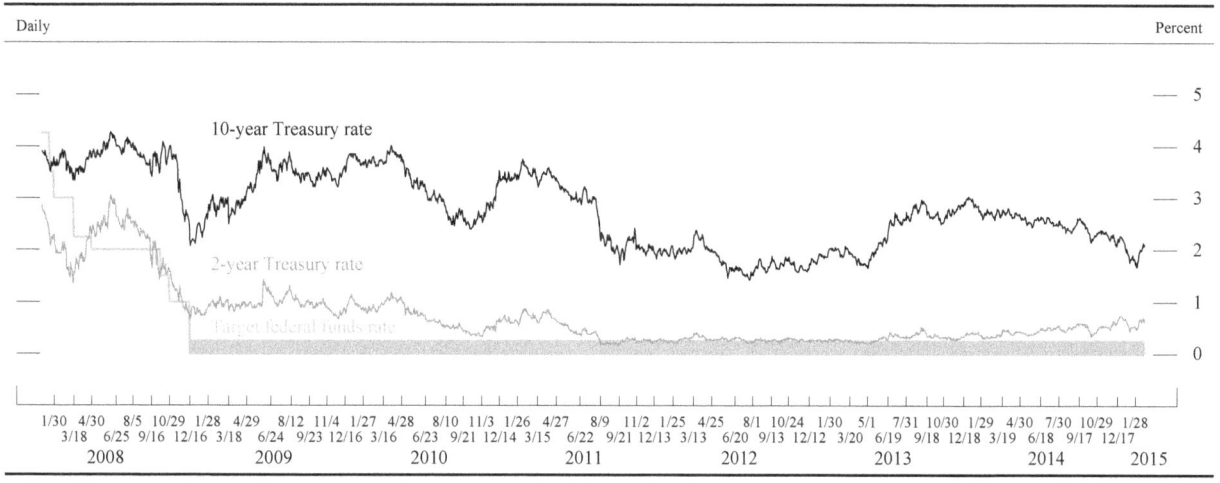

NOTE: The 2-year and 10-year Treasury rates are the constant-maturity yields based on the most actively traded securities. The dates on the horizontal axis are those of regularly scheduled Federal Open Market Committee meetings.
SOURCE: Department of the Treasury; Federal Reserve Board.

the current target range for the federal funds rate for a considerable time following the end of the asset purchase program, especially if projected inflation continued to run below the Committee's 2 percent longer-run goal and provided that longer-term inflation expectations remained well anchored.

In light of the conclusion of the asset purchase program at the end of October and the further progress that the economy had made toward the Committee's objectives, the FOMC updated its forward guidance at its December meeting. In particular, the Committee stated that it can be patient in beginning to normalize the stance of monetary policy, but it also emphasized that the Committee saw the revised language as consistent with the guidance in its previous statement.[5] The Committee restated the updated forward guidance following its January meeting based on its assessment of the economic information available at that time.[6]

In her December press conference, Chair Yellen emphasized that the update to the forward guidance did not signify a change in the Committee's policy intentions, but rather was a better reflection of the Committee's focus on the economic conditions that would make an increase in the federal funds rate appropriate.[7] Chair Yellen additionally indicated that, consistent with the new language, the Committee was unlikely to begin the normalization process for at least the following two meetings. There are a range of views within the Committee regarding the appropriate timing of the first increase in the federal funds rate, in part reflecting differences in participants' expectations for how the economy would evolve. By the time of liftoff, the Committee expects some further decline in the unemployment rate and additional improvement in labor market conditions. In addition, the Committee anticipates that, on the basis of incoming data, it will be reasonably confident that inflation will move back over the medium term to its 2 percent objective.

5. See Board of Governors of the Federal Reserve System (2014), "Federal Reserve Issues FOMC Statement," press release, December 17, www.federalreserve.gov/newsevents/press/monetary/20141217a.htm.

6. See Board of Governors of the Federal Reserve System (2015), "Federal Reserve Issues FOMC Statement," press release, January 28, www.federalreserve.gov/newsevents/press/monetary/20150128a.htm.

7. See Board of Governors of the Federal Reserve System (2014), "Transcript of Chair Yellen's FOMC Press Conference," December 17, www.federalreserve.gov/mediacenter/files/FOMCpresconf20141217.pdf.

The Committee has reiterated that, when it decides to begin to remove policy accommodation, it will take a balanced approach consistent with its longer-run goals of maximum employment and inflation of 2 percent. In addition, the Committee continues to anticipate that, even after employment and inflation are near mandate-consistent levels, economic conditions may, for some time, warrant keeping the target federal funds rate below levels the Committee views as normal in the longer run. As emphasized by Chair Yellen in her recent press conferences, FOMC participants provide a number of explanations for this view, with many citing the residual effects of the financial crisis. These effects are expected to ease gradually, but they are seen as likely to continue to constrain household spending for some time.

The FOMC has stressed the data-dependent nature of its policy stance and indicated that if incoming information signals faster progress than the Committee expects, increases in the target range for the federal funds rate will likely occur sooner than the Committee anticipates. The FOMC also stated that in the case of slower-than-expected progress, increases in the target range will likely occur later than anticipated.

The size of the Federal Reserve's balance sheet stabilized with the conclusion of the asset purchase program

After the conclusion of the large-scale asset purchase program at the end of October, the Federal Reserve's total assets stabilized at around $4.5 trillion (figure 41). As a result of the asset purchases over the second half of 2014, before the completion of the program, holdings of U.S. Treasury securities in the System Open Market Account (SOMA) increased $56 billion to $2.5 trillion, and holdings of agency debt and agency MBS increased $78 billion to $1.8 trillion on net. On the liability side of the balance sheet, the increase in the Federal Reserve's assets was largely matched by increases in currency in circulation and reverse repurchase agreements.

Given the Federal Reserve's large securities holdings, interest income on the SOMA portfolio continued to support substantial remittances to the U.S. Treasury Department. Preliminary estimates suggest that the Federal

41. Federal Reserve assets and liabilities

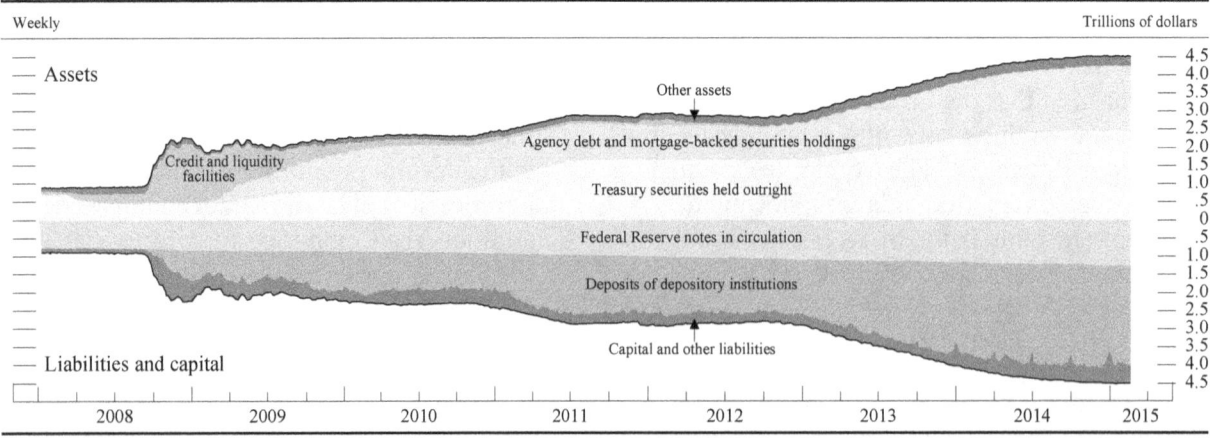

NOTE: "Credit and liquidity facilities" consists of primary, secondary, and seasonal credit; term auction credit; central bank liquidity swaps; support for Maiden Lane, Bear Stearns, and AIG; and other credit facilities, including the Primary Dealer Credit Facility, the Asset-Backed Commercial Paper Money Market Mutual Fund Liquidity Facility, the Commercial Paper Funding Facility, and the Term Asset-Backed Securities Loan Facility. "Other assets" includes unamortized premiums and discounts on securities held outright. "Capital and other liabilities" includes reverse repurchase agreements, the U.S. Treasury General Account, and the U.S. Treasury Supplementary Financing Account. Data extend through February 18, 2015.

SOURCE: Federal Reserve Board, Statistical Release H.4.1, "Factors Affecting Reserve Balances."

Reserve provided more than $98 billion of such distributions to the Treasury in 2014 and about $500 billion on a cumulative basis since 2008.[8]

The FOMC continued to plan for the eventual normalization of monetary policy . . .

FOMC meeting participants have had ongoing discussions of issues associated with the eventual normalization of the stance and conduct of monetary policy as part of prudent planning.[9] The discussions involved various tools that could be used to control the level of short-term interest rates, even while the balance sheet of the Federal Reserve remains very large, as well as approaches to normalizing the size and composition of the Federal Reserve's balance sheet.

To inform the public about its approach to normalization and to convey the Committee's confidence in its plans, the FOMC issued a statement regarding its intentions for the eventual normalization of policy following its September meeting. (That statement is reproduced in the box "Policy Normalization Principles and Plans.") As was the case before the crisis, the Committee intends to adjust the stance of monetary policy during normalization primarily through actions that influence the level of the federal funds rate and other short-term interest rates. Regarding the balance sheet, the Committee intends to reduce securities holdings in a gradual and predictable manner primarily by ceasing to reinvest repayments of principal on securities held in the SOMA. The Committee noted that economic and financial conditions could change, and that it was prepared to make adjustments to its normalization plans if warranted.

. . . including by testing the policy tools to be used

The Federal Reserve has continued to test the operational readiness of its policy tools, conducting daily overnight reverse repurchase agreement (ON RRP) operations, a series of term RRP operations, and several tests of the Term Deposit Facility. To date, testing has progressed smoothly, and short-term market rates have generally traded above the ON RRP rate, which suggests that the facility will be a useful supplementary tool for the FOMC to use in addition to the interest rate it pays on excess reserves (the IOER rate) to control the federal funds rate during the normalization process. Overall, testing operations reinforced the Federal Reserve's confidence in its view that it has the tools necessary to tighten policy at the appropriate time. (For more discussion of the Federal Reserve's preparations for the eventual normalization of monetary policy, see the box "Additional Testing of Monetary Policy Tools.")

8. See Board of Governors of the Federal Reserve System (2015), "Reserve Bank Income and Expense Data and Transfers to the Treasury for 2014," press release, January 9, www.federalreserve.gov/newsevents/press/other/20150109a.htm.

9. See Board of Governors of the Federal Reserve System (2014), "Minutes of the Federal Open Market Committee, July 29–30, 2014," press release, August 20, www.federalreserve.gov/newsevents/press/monetary/20140820a.htm.

Policy Normalization Principles and Plans

During its recent meetings, the Federal Open Market Committee (FOMC) discussed ways to normalize the stance of monetary policy and the Federal Reserve's securities holdings. The discussions were part of prudent planning and do not imply that normalization will necessarily begin soon. The Committee continues to judge that many of the normalization principles that it adopted in June 2011 remain applicable. However, in light of the changes in the System Open Market Account (SOMA) portfolio since 2011 and enhancements in the tools the Committee will have available to implement policy during normalization, the Committee has concluded that some aspects of the eventual normalization process will likely differ from those specified earlier. The Committee also has agreed that it is appropriate at this time to provide additional information regarding its normalization plans. All FOMC participants but one agreed on the following key elements of the approach they intend to implement when it becomes appropriate to begin normalizing the stance of monetary policy:

- The Committee will determine the timing and pace of policy normalization—meaning steps to raise the federal funds rate and other short-term interest rates to more normal levels and to reduce the Federal Reserve's securities holdings—so as to promote its statutory mandate of maximum employment and price stability.
  - o When economic conditions and the economic outlook warrant a less accommodative monetary policy, the Committee will raise its target range for the federal funds rate.
  - o During normalization, the Federal Reserve intends to move the federal funds rate into the target range set by the FOMC primarily by adjusting the interest rate it pays on excess reserve balances.
  - o During normalization, the Federal Reserve intends to use an overnight reverse repurchase agreement facility and other

supplementary tools as needed to help control the federal funds rate. The Committee will use an overnight reverse repurchase agreement facility only to the extent necessary and will phase it out when it is no longer needed to help control the federal funds rate.
- The Committee intends to reduce the Federal Reserve's securities holdings in a gradual and predictable manner primarily by ceasing to reinvest repayments of principal on securities held in the SOMA.
  - o The Committee expects to cease or commence phasing out reinvestments after it begins increasing the target range for the federal funds rate; the timing will depend on how economic and financial conditions and the economic outlook evolve.
  - o The Committee currently does not anticipate selling agency mortgage-backed securities as part of the normalization process, although limited sales might be warranted in the longer run to reduce or eliminate residual holdings. The timing and pace of any sales would be communicated to the public in advance.
- The Committee intends that the Federal Reserve will, in the longer run, hold no more securities than necessary to implement monetary policy efficiently and effectively, and that it will hold primarily Treasury securities, thereby minimizing the effect of Federal Reserve holdings on the allocation of credit across sectors of the economy.
- The Committee is prepared to adjust the details of its approach to policy normalization in light of economic and financial developments.

NOTE: See Board of Governors of the Federal Reserve System (2014), "Federal Reserve Issues FOMC Statement on Policy Normalization Principles and Plans," press release, September 17, www.federalreserve.gov/newsevents/press/monetary/20140917c.htm.

Additional Testing of Monetary Policy Tools

The size of the Federal Reserve's balance sheet stands at about $4.5 trillion, and reserve balances in the banking system are close to $2.5 trillion, an extraordinarily elevated level relative to the average level of reserve balances prior to the onset of the financial crisis—about $25 billion. As a result, when the Federal Open Market Committee (FOMC) eventually chooses to begin removing policy accommodation, it will do so with a level of reserves in the banking system far in excess of that during any prior period of policy tightening. As noted in the previous *Monetary Policy Report*, the Federal Reserve's elevated balance sheet implies that the traditional mechanism for tightening policy will not be feasible.[1]

As discussed in its Policy Normalization Principles and Plans, the Federal Reserve intends to move the federal funds rate into the target range set by the FOMC primarily by adjusting the interest rate it pays on excess reserve balances (the IOER rate). During policy normalization, the Federal Reserve also intends to use an overnight reverse repurchase agreement (ON RRP) facility and other supplementary tools—including term reverse repurchase agreements (term RRPs) and term deposits offered through the Term Deposit Facility (TDF)—as needed to help control the federal funds rate. As part of prudent planning, the Federal Reserve continued to test the operational readiness of these tools over the past several months, with testing evolving in terms of the offering formats, tenors and rates offered, maximum awards or allotment amounts, and eligible counterparties.[2]

With respect to RRP operations, the Federal Reserve has continued to conduct daily overnight operations

and began to conduct term operations. The testing of different formats for the ON RRP operations aimed to enhance the FOMC's understanding of how an ON RRP facility might be structured to best balance the objective of supporting monetary control with those of limiting the Federal Reserve's role in financial intermediation and mitigating potential financial stability risks the facility might pose during periods of stress.[3] In addition, the spread between the ON RRP rate and the IOER rate was varied to provide the FOMC with information about the effect of that spread on money markets and the demand for ON RRPs.

With these considerations in mind, at its September meeting, the FOMC approved changes in the ON RRP exercise that included raising the counterparty-specific limit from $10 billion to $30 billion, limiting the overall size of each operation to $300 billion, and introducing an auction process that would be used to determine the interest rate and allocate take-up if the sum of bids exceeded the overall limit. In addition, during the fourth quarter of 2014, the FOMC approved further changes in the exercise under which the offering rate at the ON RRP operations was varied between 3 and 10 basis points. Participation in and usage of ON RRPs fluctuated from day to day, reflecting changes in the spread between market rates and the ON RRP rate as well as quarter-end and year-end dynamics (figure A). The limit on the overall size of the operation did not bind except at the end of the third quarter.[4] Increases in ON RRP offered rates appeared to put some upward pressure on unsecured money market rates, as anticipated, and the offered rate continued to provide a soft floor for secured rates. Changes in the ON RRP offered rate induced changes in the spread between the IOER rate of 25 basis points and the ON RRP offered rate for those days. Those changes did not appear to affect the volume of activity in the federal funds market.

The term RRP operations approved for the end of 2014 were aimed at providing the FOMC with information about the potential effectiveness of this supplementary policy tool in helping to control

---

1. For further discussion of how the alternative policy tools affect a range of short-term interest rates, see the box "Planning for Monetary Policy Implementation during Normalization" in Board of Governors of the Federal Reserve System (2014), *Monetary Policy Report* (Washington: Board of Governors, July), www.federalreserve.gov/monetarypolicy/mpr_20140715_part2.htm.

2. The types of counterparties that are currently eligible to participate in the Federal Reserve's ON RRP operations include depository institutions, money market funds, government-sponsored enterprises, and primary dealers, while only depository institutions may participate in TDF operations. At its December 2014 meeting, the FOMC reauthorized the ON RRP test operations through January 29, 2016. On January 16, 2015, the Federal Reserve Bank of New York announced the addition of 25 RRP counterparties, bringing the total number of counterparties to 164. These newly added counterparties are currently in the process of finalizing the operational details. Results of RRP operations can be found on the Federal Reserve Bank of New York's website at www.newyorkfed.org/markets/omo/dmm/temp.cfm, and results of the TDF operations can be found on the Federal Reserve Board's website at www.federalreserve.gov/monetarypolicy/tdf.htm.

3. For a discussion of issues related to the use of ON RRPs as a supplementary tool during normalization, see Josh Frost, Lorie Logan, Antoine Martin, Patrick McCabe, Fabio Natalucci and Julie Remache (2015), "Overnight RRP Operations as a Monetary Policy Tool: Some Design Considerations," Finance and Economics Discussion Series 2015-010 (Washington: Board of Governors of the Federal Reserve System, February), www.federalreserve.gov/econresdata/feds/2015/files/2015010pap.pdf.

4. As term RRP operations crossing year-end were conducted in addition to ON RRP operations, the limit on the overall size of the ON RRP operations did not bind at year-end.

the federal funds rate, particularly when there are significant and transitory shifts in money market activity, such as over quarter- and year-ends. To this end, the Federal Reserve conducted term RRP operations on December 8, 15, 22, and 29, with offering amounts of $50 billion for each of the first two operations and $100 billion for each of the latter two operations.[5] Although the first two term auctions were oversubscribed, the third and fourth term operations were undersubscribed. Overall, the ON RRP and term RRP operations appeared to ease downside rate pressures in money markets over year-end, and the unwinding of all four term operations on January 5, 2015, was orderly. The Federal Reserve will conduct a further test of term RRPs over quarter-ends with a series of term RRP operations spanning the March 2015 quarter-end. Also, to help advance its understanding of how term RRPs could help to control the federal funds rate, the Federal Reserve has begun a series of four term RRP test operations that do not span a quarter-end date. The first two of these operations were conducted on February 12 and on February 19. Both operations were oversubscribed, and the awarded interest rate on these two term RRPs was in line with the awarded rate on concurrent ON RRP operations.

The Federal Reserve's testing of the TDF also continued to evolve in the second half of 2014 and early 2015, with the aim of increasing participation by depository institutions as well as improving operational readiness. Since the previous *Monetary Policy Report*, the Federal Reserve conducted two series of TDF test operations. In the second half of 2014, a series of eight TDF test operations included an early withdrawal feature that allowed depository institutions to withdraw funds held in term deposits on payment of an early withdrawal penalty.[6] The maximum award amount per institution and the interest rate paid on term deposits offered through the facility were raised gradually over the course of the series in a manner broadly similar to the series of test operations conducted earlier in the year that did not include an early withdrawal feature. The level of activity increased considerably relative to the earlier test operations, with take-up reaching just over $400 billion at the final operation and nearly 100 depository institutions participating (figure B). In the second series of test operations, held in February 2015, the Federal Reserve conducted a series of weekly TDF operations offering 21-day term deposits that settled on the same day the operation was executed, eliminating the 3-day lag between the execution of an operation and settlement in previous tests. On net, the series results provide additional evidence that significant take-up can occur at a few basis points over the IOER rate even for longer terms.

---

5. For details on the format of these operations, see the December 1, 2014, Statement Regarding Term Reverse Repurchase Agreements on the Federal Reserve Bank of New York's website at www.newyorkfed.org/markets/opolicy/operating_policy_141201.html.

6. The early withdrawal option makes such deposits eligible to meet requirements under the Basel III Liquidity Coverage Ratio.

A.   Reverse repurchase agreement operations

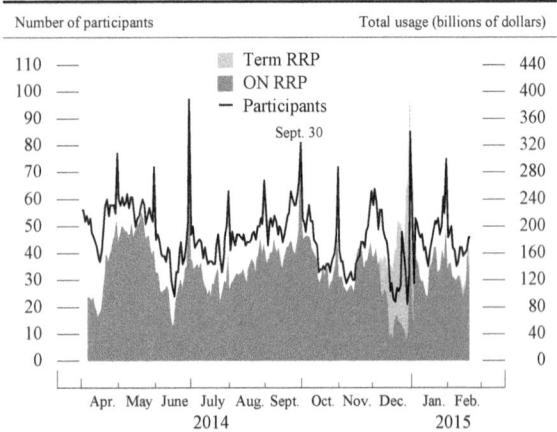

NOTE: ON RRP is overnight reverse repurchase agreement.
On September 30, 2014, ON RRP bids were $407 billion and allotments were $300 billion.
SOURCE: Federal Reserve Bank of New York, temporary open market operations data.

B.   Term Deposit Facility operations

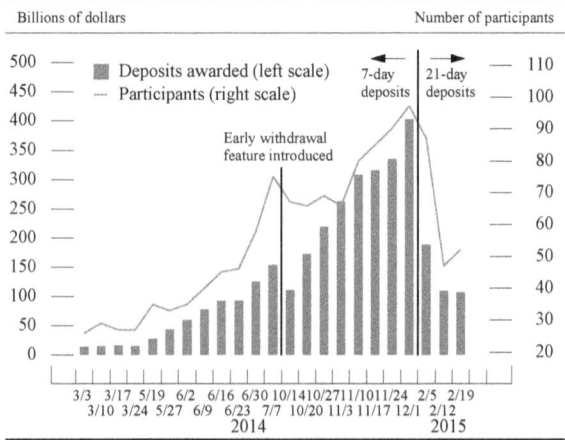

SOURCE: Federal Reserve Board.

PART 3
SUMMARY OF ECONOMIC PROJECTIONS

The following material appeared as an addendum to the minutes of the December 16–17, 2014, meeting of the Federal Open Market Committee.

In conjunction with the Federal Open Market Committee (FOMC) meeting held on December 16–17, 2014, meeting participants submitted their projections of the most likely outcomes for real output growth, the unemployment rate, inflation, and the federal funds rate for each year from 2014 to 2017 and over the longer run.[10] Each participant's projection was based on information available at the time of the meeting plus his or her assessment of appropriate monetary policy and assumptions about the factors likely

to affect economic outcomes. The longer-run projections represent each participant's assessment of the value to which each variable would be expected to converge, over time, under appropriate monetary policy and in the absence of further shocks to the economy. "Appropriate monetary policy" is defined as the future path of policy that each participant deems most likely to foster outcomes for economic activity and inflation that best satisfy his or her individual interpretation of the Federal Reserve's objectives of maximum employment and stable prices.

---

10. As discussed in its Policy Normalization Principles and Plans, released on September 17, 2014, the Committee intends to target a range for the federal funds rate during normalization. Participants were asked to provide, in their contributions to the Summary of Economic Projections, either the midpoint of the target range for the federal funds rate for any period when a range was anticipated or the target level for the federal funds rate, as appropriate. In the lower panel of figure 2, these values have been rounded to the nearest $\frac{1}{8}$ percentage point.

Overall, FOMC participants expected that, after a slowdown in the first half of 2014, economic growth under appropriate policy would be faster in the second half of 2014 and over 2015 and 2016 than their estimates of the U.S. economy's longer-run normal growth rate. On balance, participants then saw economic growth moving back toward their assessments of its longer-run pace in 2017 (table 1 and figure 1). Most participants projected that the

Table 1. Economic projections of Federal Reserve Board members and Federal Reserve Bank presidents, December 2014
Percent

Variable	Central tendency[1]					Range[2]				
	2014	2015	2016	2017	Longer run	2014	2015	2016	2017	Longer run
Change in real GDP........	2.3 to 2.4	2.6 to 3.0	2.5 to 3.0	2.3 to 2.5	2.0 to 2.3	2.3 to 2.5	2.1 to 3.2	2.1 to 3.0	2.0 to 2.7	1.8 to 2.7
September projection	2.0 to 2.2	2.6 to 3.0	2.6 to 2.9	2.3 to 2.5	2.0 to 2.3	1.8 to 2.3	2.1 to 3.2	2.1 to 3.0	2.0 to 2.6	1.8 to 2.6
Unemployment rate	5.8	5.2 to 5.3	5.0 to 5.2	4.9 to 5.3	5.2 to 5.5	5.7 to 5.8	5.0 to 5.5	4.9 to 5.4	4.7 to 5.7	5.0 to 5.8
September projection	5.9 to 6.0	5.4 to 5.6	5.1 to 5.4	4.9 to 5.3	5.2 to 5.5	5.7 to 6.1	5.2 to 5.7	4.9 to 5.6	4.7 to 5.8	5.0 to 6.0
PCE inflation	1.2 to 1.3	1.0 to 1.6	1.7 to 2.0	1.8 to 2.0	2.0	1.2 to 1.6	1.0 to 2.2	1.6 to 2.1	1.8 to 2.2	2.0
September projection	1.5 to 1.7	1.6 to 1.9	1.7 to 2.0	1.9 to 2.0	2.0	1.5 to 1.8	1.5 to 2.4	1.6 to 2.1	1.7 to 2.2	2.0
Core PCE inflation[3]	1.5 to 1.6	1.5 to 1.8	1.7 to 2.0	1.8 to 2.0		1.5 to 1.6	1.5 to 2.2	1.6 to 2.1	1.8 to 2.2	
September projection	1.5 to 1.6	1.6 to 1.9	1.8 to 2.0	1.9 to 2.0		1.5 to 1.8	1.6 to 2.4	1.7 to 2.2	1.8 to 2.2	

NOTE: Projections of change in real gross domestic product (GDP) and projections for both measures of inflation are percent changes from the fourth quarter of the previous year to the fourth quarter of the year indicated. PCE inflation and core PCE inflation are the percentage rates of change in, respectively, the price index for personal consumption expenditures (PCE) and the price index for PCE excluding food and energy. Projections for the unemployment rate are for the average civilian unemployment rate in the fourth quarter of the year indicated. Each participant's projections are based on his or her assessment of appropriate monetary policy. Longer-run projections represent each participant's assessment of the rate to which each variable would be expected to converge under appropriate monetary policy and in the absence of further shocks to the economy. The September projections were made in conjunction with the meeting of the Federal Open Market Committee on September 16–17, 2014.

1. The central tendency excludes the three highest and three lowest projections for each variable in each year.
2. The range for a variable in a given year includes all participants' projections, from lowest to highest, for that variable in that year.
3. Longer-run projections for core PCE inflation are not collected.

Figure 1. Central tendencies and ranges of economic projections, 2014–17 and over the longer run

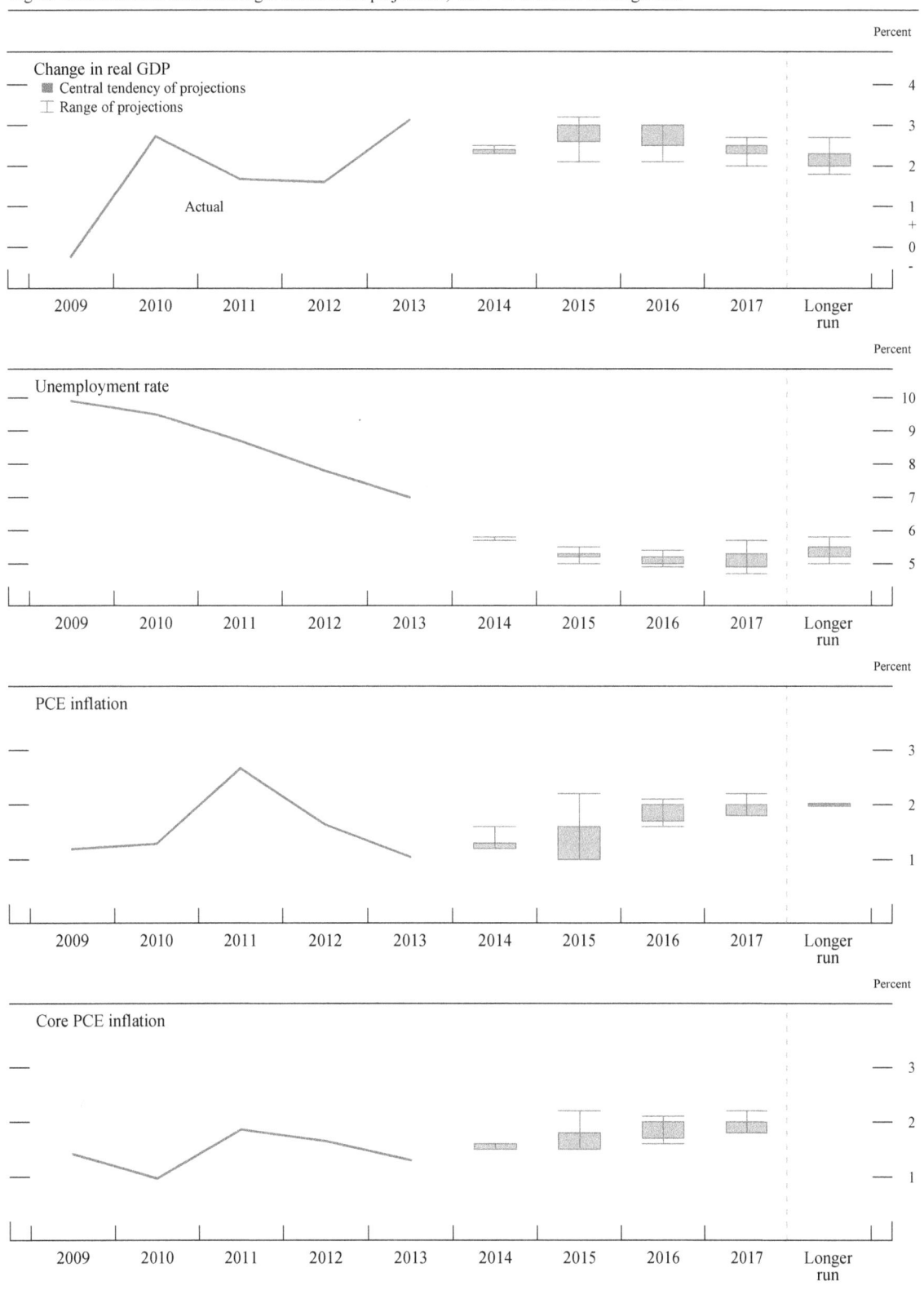

NOTE: Definitions of variables are in the general note to table 1. The data for the actual values of the variables are annual.

unemployment rate will continue to decline in 2015 and 2016, and all participants projected that the unemployment rate will be at or below their individual judgments of its longer-run normal level by the end of 2016. All participants projected that inflation, as measured by the four-quarter change in the price index for personal consumption expenditures (PCE), would rise gradually, on balance, over the next few years. Most participants saw inflation approaching the Committee's 2 percent longer-run objective in 2016 and 2017. While a few participants projected that inflation would rise temporarily above 2 percent during the forecast period, many others expected inflation to remain low through 2017.

Participants judged that it would be appropriate to begin raising the target range for the federal funds rate over the projection period as labor market indicators and inflation move back toward values the Committee judges consistent with the attainment of its mandated objectives of maximum employment and stable prices. As shown in figure 2, all but a couple of participants anticipated that it would be appropriate to begin raising the target range for the federal funds rate in 2015, with most projecting that it will be appropriate to raise the target federal funds rate fairly gradually.

Most participants viewed the uncertainty associated with their outlooks for economic growth and the unemployment rate as broadly similar to the average level of the past 20 years. Most participants also judged the level of uncertainty about inflation to be broadly similar to the average level of the past 20 years, although a few participants viewed it as higher. In addition, most participants continued to see the risks to the outlook for economic growth and for the unemployment rate as broadly balanced. A majority saw the risks to inflation as broadly balanced; however, a number of participants saw the risks to inflation as weighted to the downside, while one judged these risks as tilted to the upside.

The Outlook for Economic Activity

Participants projected that, conditional on their individual assumptions about appropriate monetary policy, growth in real gross domestic product (GDP) would pick up from its low level in the first half of 2014 and run above their estimates of its longer-run normal rate in the second half of 2014 and over 2015 and 2016. Participants pointed to a number of factors that they expected would contribute to stronger real output growth, including improving labor market conditions, lower energy prices, rising household net worth, diminishing restraint from fiscal policy, and highly accommodative monetary policy. On balance, participants saw real GDP growth moving back toward, but remaining at or somewhat above, its longer-run rate in 2017 as monetary policy adjusts appropriately.

In general, participants' revisions to their forecasts for real GDP growth relative to their projections for the September meeting were modest. However, all participants revised up their projections of real GDP growth somewhat for 2014, with a number of them noting that recent data releases regarding real economic activity had been stronger than anticipated. The central tendencies of participants' current projections for real GDP growth were 2.3 to 2.4 percent in 2014, 2.6 to 3.0 percent in 2015, 2.5 to 3.0 percent in 2016, and 2.3 to 2.5 percent in 2017. The central tendency of the projections of real GDP growth over the longer run was 2.0 to 2.3 percent, unchanged from September.

All participants projected that the unemployment rate will decline, on balance, through 2016, and all participants projected that, by the end of that year, the unemployment rate will be at or below their individual judgments of its longer-run normal level. The central tendencies of participants' forecasts for the unemployment rate in the fourth quarter of each year were 5.8 percent in 2014, 5.2 to 5.3 percent in 2015, 5.0 to 5.2 percent in 2016, and 4.9 to 5.3 percent

Figure 2. Overview of FOMC participants' assessments of appropriate monetary policy

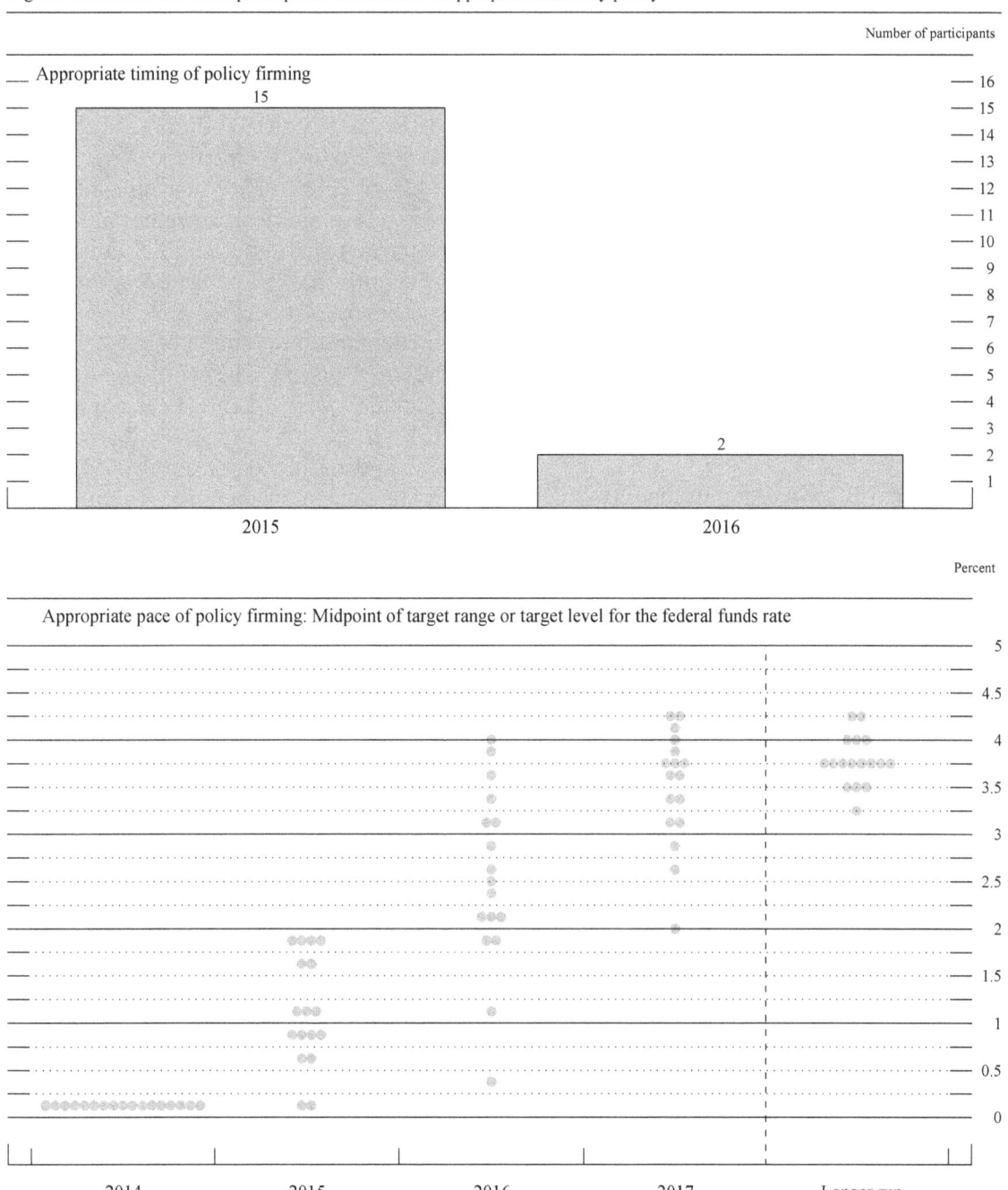

NOTE: In the upper panel, the height of each bar denotes the number of FOMC participants who judge that, under appropriate monetary policy, the first increase in the target range for the federal funds rate from its current range of 0 to ¼ percent will occur in the specified calendar year. In September 2014, the numbers of FOMC participants who judged that the first increase in the target federal funds rate would occur in 2014, 2015, and 2016 were, respectively, 1, 14, and 2. In the lower panel, each shaded circle indicates the value (rounded to the nearest ˜ percentage point) of an individual participant' s judgment of the midpoint of the appropriate target range for the federal funds rate or the appropriate target level for the federal funds rate at the end of the specified calendar year or over the longer run.

in 2017. Almost all participants' projected paths for the unemployment rate shifted down slightly through 2015 compared with their projections in September; many participants noted that recent data pointing to improving labor market conditions were an important factor underlying the downward revisions in their unemployment rate forecasts. The central tendency of participants' estimates of the longer-run normal rate of unemployment that would prevail under appropriate monetary policy and in the absence of further shocks to the economy was unchanged at 5.2 to 5.5 percent; the range of these estimates was 5.0 to 5.8 percent, down slightly from 5.0 to 6.0 percent in September.

Figures 3.A and 3.B show that participants held a range of views regarding the likely outcomes for real GDP growth and the unemployment rate through 2017. Some of the diversity of views reflected their individual assessments of the effects of lower oil prices on consumer spending and business investment, of the rate at which the forces that have been restraining the pace of the economic recovery would continue to abate, of the trajectory for growth in consumption as labor market slack diminishes, and of the appropriate path of monetary policy. Relative to September, the dispersion of participants' projections for real GDP growth was little changed from 2015 to 2017, while for the unemployment rate, the dispersion was a bit narrower.

The Outlook for Inflation

Compared with September, the central tendencies of participants' projections for PCE inflation under the assumption of appropriate monetary policy moved down for 2014 and 2015 but were largely unchanged for 2016 and 2017. In commenting on the changes to their projections, many participants indicated that the significant decline in energy prices and the appreciation of the dollar since the Committee's September

meeting likely will put temporary downward pressure on inflation. The central tendencies of participants' projections for core PCE inflation moved down somewhat for 2015 but were mostly unchanged in other years. Almost all participants projected that PCE inflation would rise gradually, on balance, over the period from 2015 to 2017, reaching a level at or near the Committee's 2 percent objective. A few participants expected PCE inflation to rise slightly above 2 percent at some point during the forecast period, while many others expected inflation to remain below 2 percent for the entire period. The central tendencies for PCE inflation were 1.2 to 1.3 percent in 2014, 1.0 to 1.6 percent in 2015, 1.7 to 2.0 percent in 2016, and 1.8 to 2.0 percent in 2017. The central tendencies of the forecasts for core inflation were higher than those for the headline measure in 2014 and 2015, reflecting the effects of lower oil prices. The central tendencies of the two measures were equal in 2016 and in 2017. Factors cited by participants as likely to contribute to a gradual rise of inflation toward the Committee's longer-run objective of 2 percent included stable longer-term inflation expectations, steadily diminishing resource slack, a pickup in wage growth, waning effects of declines in oil prices, and still-accommodative monetary policy.

Figures 3.C and 3.D provide information on the diversity of participants' views about the outlook for inflation. In addition to moving lower, the range of participants' projections for PCE inflation in 2015 widened somewhat relative to September, likely reflecting in part differences in participants' assessments of the effects of the recent decline in energy prices on the outlook for inflation. The ranges for core inflation narrowed in 2014 and 2015. In other years of the projection, the ranges of the inflation projections were relatively little changed. The range for both measures in 2017 continued to show a very substantial concentration near the Committee's 2 percent longer-run objective by that time.

Figure 3.A. Distribution of participants' projections for the change in real GDP, 2014–17 and over the longer run

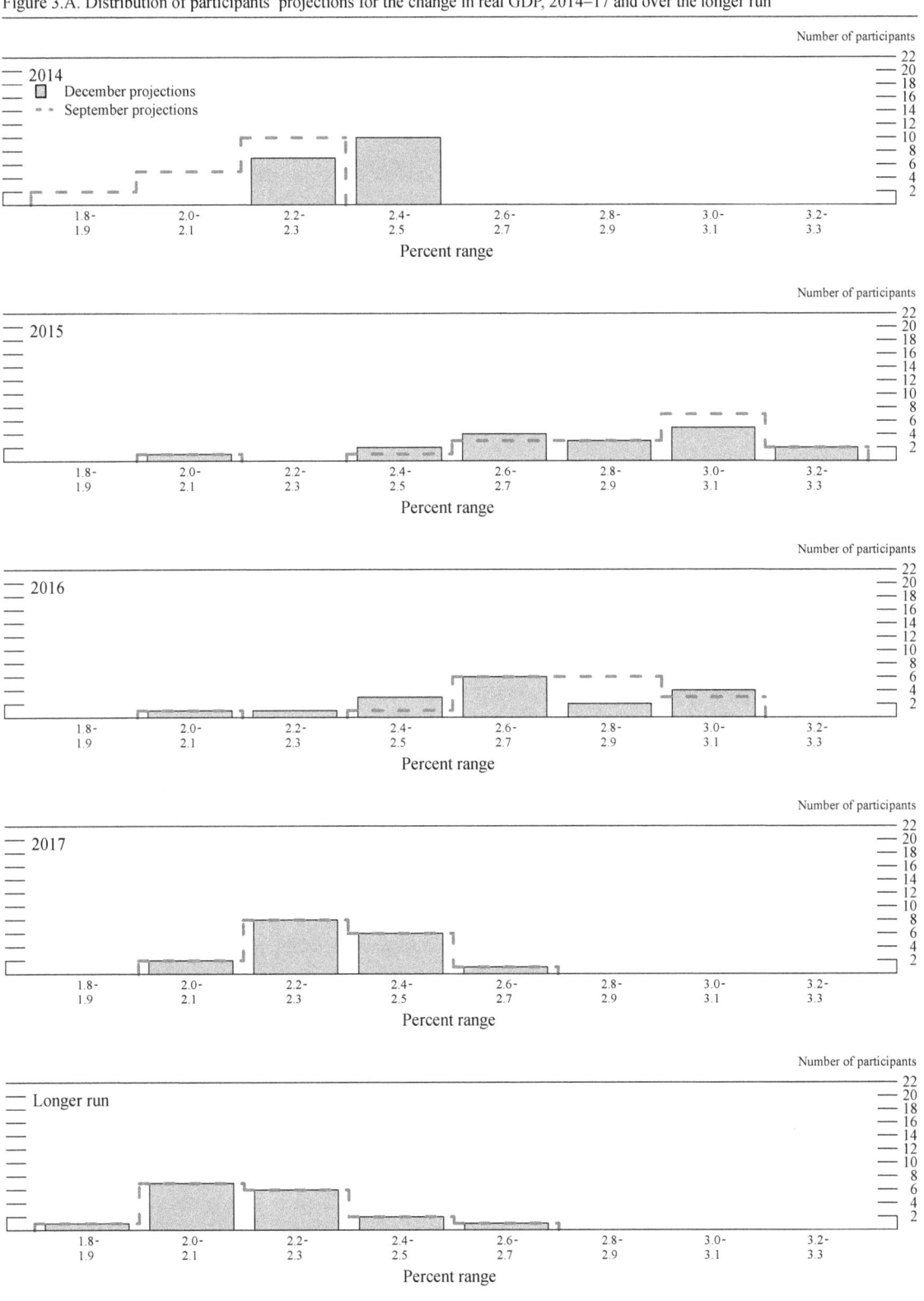

NOTE: Definitions of variables are in the general note to table 1.

Figure 3.B. Distribution of participants' projections for the unemployment rate, 2014–17 and over the longer run

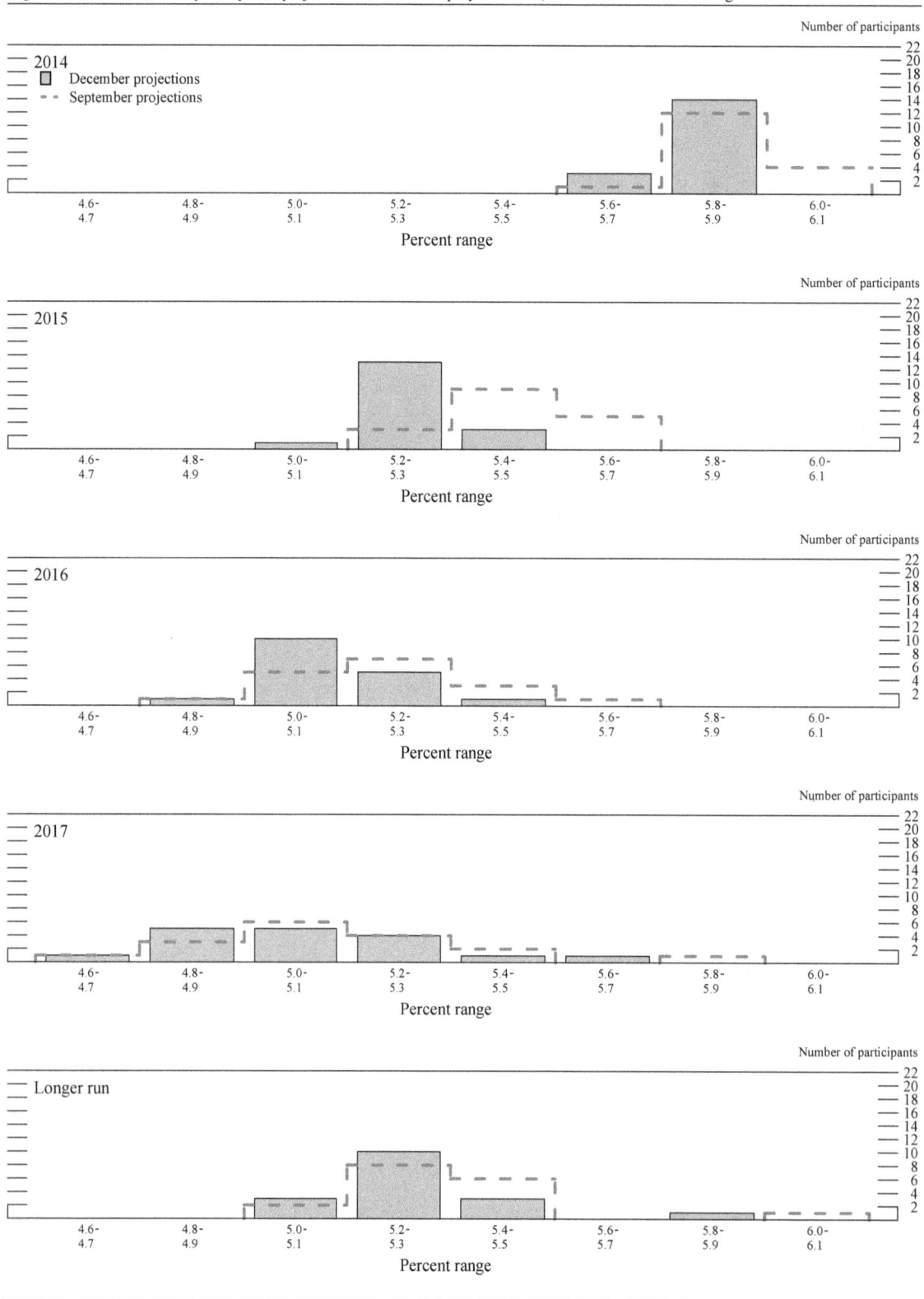

NOTE: Definitions of variables are in the general note to table 1.

Figure 3.C. Distribution of participants' projections for PCE inflation, 2014–17 and over the longer run

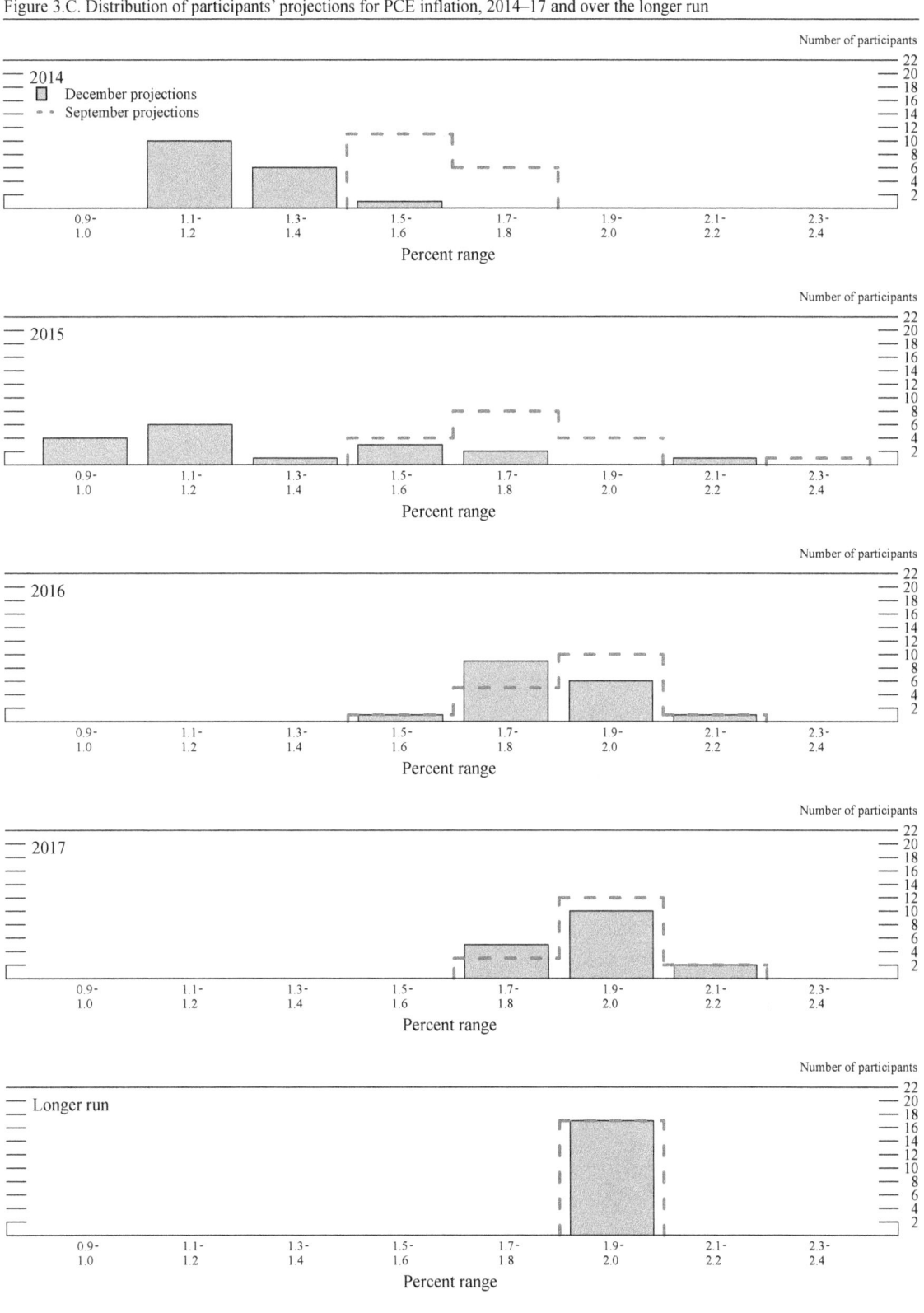

NOTE: Definitions of variables are in the general note to table 1.

Figure 3.D. Distribution of participants' projections for core PCE inflation, 2014–17

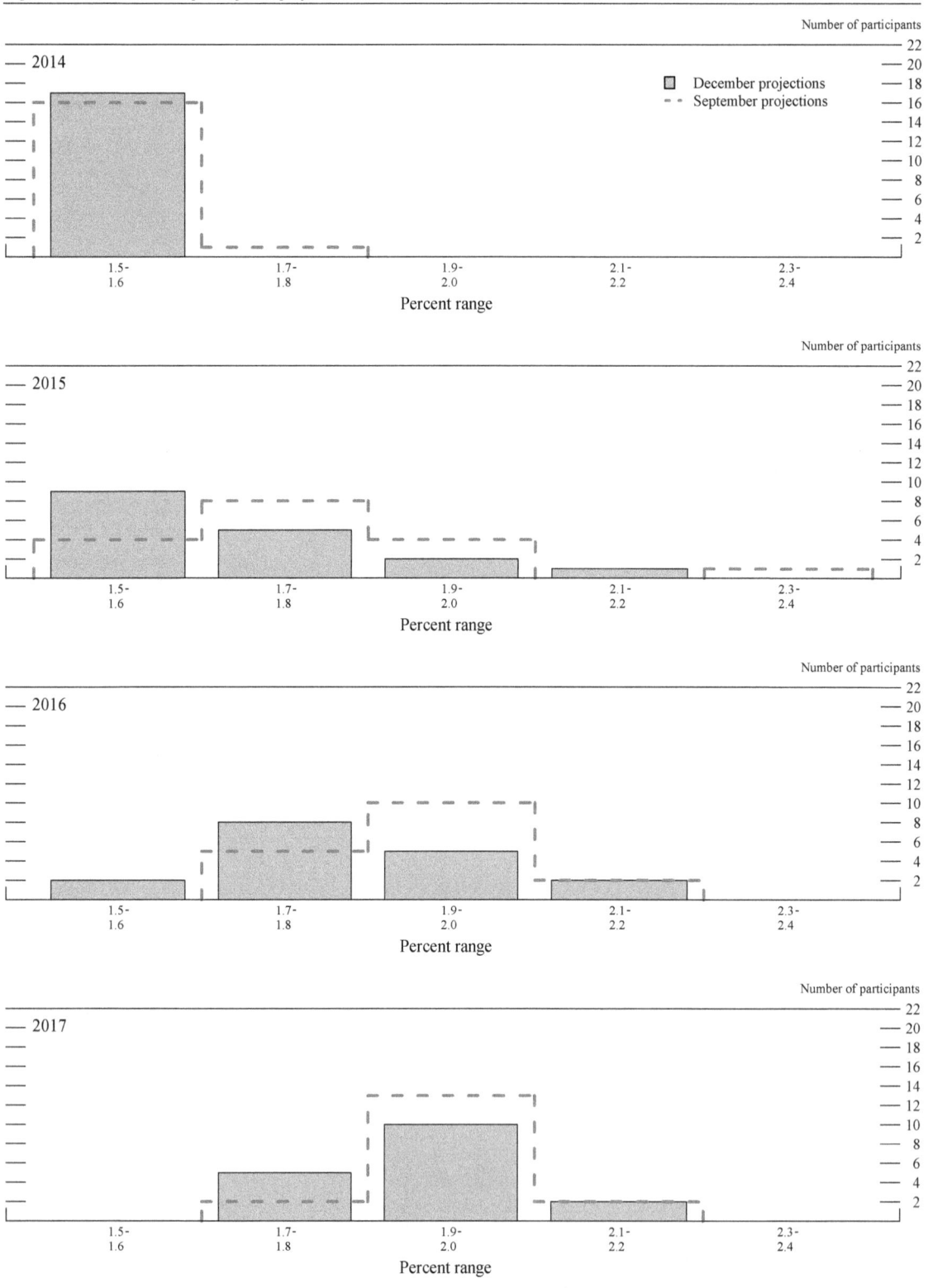

NOTE: Definitions of variables are in the general note to table 1.

Appropriate Monetary Policy

Participants judged that it would be appropriate to begin raising the target range for the federal funds rate over the projection period as labor market indicators and inflation move back toward values the Committee judges consistent with the attainment of its mandated objectives of maximum employment and price stability. As shown in figure 2, all but two participants anticipated that it would be appropriate to begin raising the target range for the federal funds rate during 2015. However, most projected that the appropriate level of the federal funds rate would remain considerably below its longer-run normal level through 2016. Most participants expected the appropriate level of the federal funds rate would be near, or already would have reached, their individual view of its longer-run normal level by the end of 2017.

All participants projected that the unemployment rate would be at or below 5.5 percent at the end of the year in which they judged the initial increase in the target range for the federal funds rate would be warranted, and all but one anticipated that inflation would be at or below the Committee's 2 percent goal at the end of that year. Most participants projected that the unemployment rate would be at or somewhat above their estimates of its longer-run normal level at that time.

Figure 3.E provides the distribution of participants' judgments regarding the appropriate level of the target federal funds rate, conditional on their assessments of the economic outlook, at the end of each calendar year from 2014 to 2017 and over the longer run. All participants judged that economic conditions would warrant maintaining the current exceptionally low level of the federal funds rate into 2015. The median values of the federal funds rate at the end of 2015 and 2016 fell 25 basis points and 38 basis points relative to September, to 1.13 percent and 2.50 percent, respectively, while the mean values fell 15 basis points for both years, to 1.13 percent in 2015

and 2.54 percent in 2016. The dispersion of the projections for the appropriate level of the federal funds rate was narrower in 2014 and 2015 and was little changed in 2016 and 2017. Most participants judged that it would be appropriate to set the federal funds rate at or near its longer-run normal level in 2017, although a number of them projected that the federal funds rate would still need to be set appreciably below its longer-run normal level at that time and one anticipated that it would be appropriate to target a level noticeably above its longer-run normal level. Participants provided a number of reasons why they thought it would be appropriate for the federal funds rate to remain below its longer-run normal level for some time after inflation and the unemployment rate were near mandate-consistent levels. These reasons included an assessment that the headwinds that have been holding back the recovery will continue to exert some restraint on economic activity at that time, that residual slack in the labor market will still be evident in other measures of labor utilization, and that the risks to the economic outlook are asymmetric as a result of the constraints on monetary policy associated with the effective lower bound on the federal funds rate.

As in September, estimates of the longer-run level of the federal funds rate ranged from 3.25 to 4.25 percent. All participants judged that inflation over the longer run would be equal to the Committee's inflation objective of 2 percent, implying that their individual judgments regarding the appropriate longer-run level of the real federal funds rate in the absence of further shocks to the economy ranged from 1.25 to 2.25 percent.

Participants' views of the appropriate path for monetary policy were informed by their judgments about the state of the economy, including the values of the unemployment rate and other labor market indicators that would be consistent with maximum employment, the extent to which the economy was currently falling short of maximum employment,

Figure 3.E. Distribution of participants' projections for the target federal funds rate, 2014–17 and over the longer run

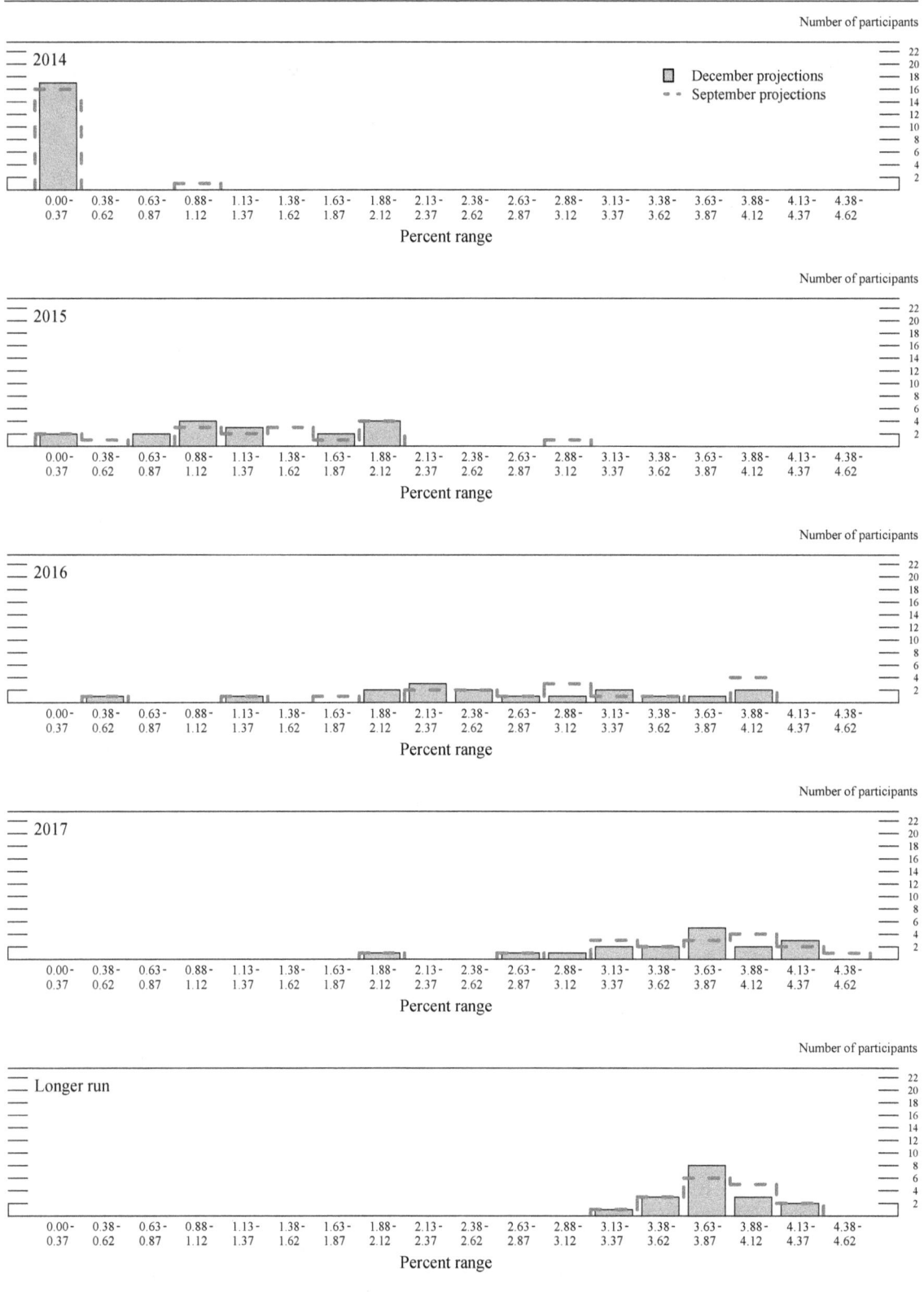

NOTE: The target federal funds rate is measured as the level of the target rate at the end of the calendar year or in the longer run.

the prospects for inflation to return to the Committee's longer-term objective of 2 percent, the desire to minimize potential disruption in financial markets by avoiding unusually rapid increases in the federal funds rate, and the balance of risks around the outlook. Some participants also mentioned the prescriptions of various monetary policy rules as factors they considered in judging the appropriate path for the federal funds rate.

Uncertainty and Risks

Nearly all participants continued to judge the levels of uncertainty attending their projections for real GDP growth and the unemployment rate as broadly similar to the norms during the previous 20 years (figure 4).[11] Most participants continued to see the risks to their outlooks for real GDP growth as broadly balanced. A few participants viewed the risks to real GDP growth as weighted to the downside; one viewed the risks as weighted to the upside. Those participants who viewed the risks as weighted to the downside cited, for example, concern about the limited ability of monetary policy at the effective lower bound to respond to further negative shocks to the economy or about the trajectory for economic growth abroad. As in September, nearly all participants judged the risks to the outlook for the unemployment rate to be broadly balanced.

---

11. Table 2 provides estimates of the forecast uncertainty for the change in real GDP, the unemployment rate, and total consumer price inflation over the period from 1994 through 2013. At the end of this summary, the box "Forecast Uncertainty" discusses the sources and interpretation of uncertainty in the economic forecasts and explains the approach used to assess the uncertainty and risks attending the participants' projections.

Table 2. Average historical projection error ranges
Percentage points

Variable	2014	2015	2016	2017
Change in real GDP[1]	±0.9	±1.8	±2.1	±2.1
Unemployment rate[1]	±0.2	±0.8	±1.4	±1.8
Total consumer prices[2]	±0.2	±0.9	±1.0	±1.0

NOTE: Error ranges shown are measured as plus or minus the root mean squared error of projections for 1994 through 2013 that were released in the winter by various private and government forecasters. As described in the box "Forecast Uncertainty," under certain assumptions, there is about a 70 percent probability that actual outcomes for real GDP, unemployment, and consumer prices will be in ranges implied by the average size of projection errors made in the past. For more information, see David Reifschneider and Peter Tulip (2007), "Gauging the Uncertainty of the Economic Outlook from Historical Forecasting Errors," Finance and Economics Discussion Series 2007-60 (Washington: Board of Governors of the Federal Reserve System, November), available at www.federalreserve.gov/pubs/feds/2007/200760/200760abs.html; and Board of Governors of the Federal Reserve System, Division of Research and Statistics (2014), "Updated Historical Forecast Errors," memorandum, April 9, www.federalreserve.gov/foia/files/20140409-historical-forecast-errors.pdf.
   1. Definitions of variables are in the general note to table 1.
   2. Measure is the overall consumer price index, the price measure that has been most widely used in government and private economic forecasts. Projection is percent change, fourth quarter of the previous year to the fourth quarter of the year indicated.

As in September, participants generally agreed that the levels of uncertainty associated with their inflation forecasts were broadly similar to historical norms, and most saw the risks to those projections as broadly balanced. A number of participants, however, viewed the risks to their inflation forecasts as tilted to the downside; the reasons discussed included the possibility that the recent low levels of inflation could prove more persistent than anticipated; the possibility that the upward pull on prices from inflation expectations might be weaker than assumed; or the judgment that, in current circumstances, it would be difficult for the Committee to respond effectively to low-inflation outcomes. Conversely, one participant saw upside risks to inflation, citing uncertainty about the timing and efficacy of the Committee's withdrawal of monetary policy accommodation.

Figure 4. Uncertainty and risks in economic projections

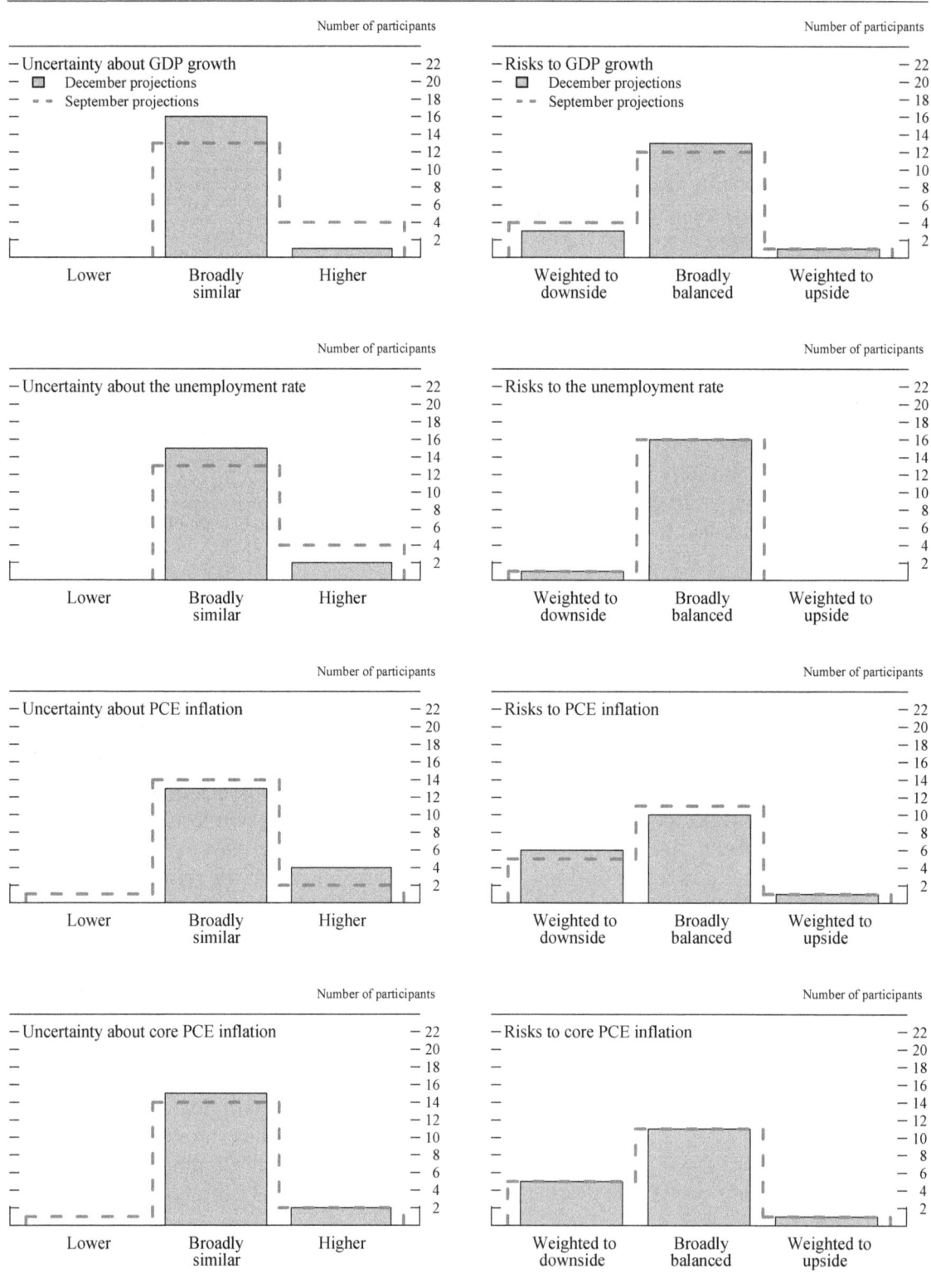

NOTE: For definitions of uncertainty and risks in economic projections, see the box "Forecast Uncertainty." Definitions of variables are in the general note to table 1.

Forecast Uncertainty

The economic projections provided by the members of the Board of Governors and the presidents of the Federal Reserve Banks inform discussions of monetary policy among policymakers and can aid public understanding of the basis for policy actions. Considerable uncertainty attends these projections, however. The economic and statistical models and relationships used to help produce economic forecasts are necessarily imperfect descriptions of the real world, and the future path of the economy can be affected by myriad unforeseen developments and events. Thus, in setting the stance of monetary policy, participants consider not only what appears to be the most likely economic outcome as embodied in their projections, but also the range of alternative possibilities, the likelihood of their occurring, and the potential costs to the economy should they occur.

Table 2 summarizes the average historical accuracy of a range of forecasts, including those reported in past *Monetary Policy Reports* and those prepared by the Federal Reserve Board's staff in advance of meetings of the Federal Open Market Committee. The projection error ranges shown in the table illustrate the considerable uncertainty associated with economic forecasts. For example, suppose a participant projects that real gross domestic product (GDP) and total consumer prices will rise steadily at annual rates of, respectively, 3 percent and 2 percent. If the uncertainty attending those projections is similar to that experienced in the past and the risks around the projections are broadly balanced, the numbers reported in table 2 would imply a probability of about 70 percent that actual GDP would expand within a range of 2.1 to 3.9 percent in the current year, 1.2 to 4.8 percent in the second year, and 0.9 to 5.1 percent in the third and fourth years. The corresponding 70 percent confidence intervals for overall inflation would be 1.8 to 2.2 percent in the current year, 1.1 to 2.9 percent in the second year, and 1.0 to 3.0 percent in the third and fourth years.

Because current conditions may differ from those that prevailed, on average, over history, participants provide judgments as to whether the uncertainty attached to their projections of each variable is greater than, smaller than, or broadly similar to typical levels of forecast uncertainty in the past, as shown in table 2. Participants also provide judgments as to whether the risks to their projections are weighted to the upside, are weighted to the downside, or are broadly balanced. That is, participants judge whether each variable is more likely to be above or below their projections of the most likely outcome. These judgments about the uncertainty and the risks attending each participant's projections are distinct from the diversity of participants' views about the most likely outcomes. Forecast uncertainty is concerned with the risks associated with a particular projection rather than with divergences across a number of different projections.

As with real activity and inflation, the outlook for the future path of the federal funds rate is subject to considerable uncertainty. This uncertainty arises primarily because each participant's assessment of the appropriate stance of monetary policy depends importantly on the evolution of real activity and inflation over time. If economic conditions evolve in an unexpected manner, then assessments of the appropriate setting of the federal funds rate would change from that point forward.

3

Abbreviations

AFE	advanced foreign economy
BHC	bank holding company
BOJ	Bank of Japan
CDS	credit default swap
C&I	commercial and industrial
ECB	European Central Bank
ECI	employment cost index
E&I	equipment and intangibles
EME	emerging market economy
FOMC	Federal Open Market Committee; also, the Committee
GDP	gross domestic product
IOER	interest on excess reserves
MBS	mortgage-backed securities
ON RRP	overnight reverse repurchase agreement
OPEC	Organization of the Petroleum Exporting Countries
PCE	personal consumption expenditures
RRP	reverse repurchase agreement
SEP	Summary of Economic Projections
SLOOS	Senior Loan Officer Opinion Survey on Bank Lending Practices
SOMA	System Open Market Account
S&P	Standard & Poor's